Iris Briggs Sharaf is British by birth and was born in 1930. She got educated in state schools, and started her work life in London at Harrods Book Department and Library then at Foyles. She married in her twenties to an Egyptian professor of geography and then immigrated to Egypt where Iris spent the greater part of her life with periods of five and four years respectively in Libya and Sudan, with extended visits to Saudi Arabia. Iris worked many years of her life at the WHO regional office in Alexandria.

Much of her writing, though by no means all, concerns the Middle East, of which she absorbed considerable knowledge. Speaking Arabic reasonably well, mixing at all levels of society in all these countries – this has facilitated her writing about them, both fiction and nonfiction.

Iris was the matriarch of a large Egyptian family, children, grandchildren and even great grandchildren. She passed away in 2016 leaving behind a list of unpublished work.

This book is dedicated
firstly, to the Lord, Who inspired and enabled me to write it and then to the
spirit of Agnes Birrell (Nancy)
'The sweetest soul that ever looked with human eyes.'

Iris Briggs Sharaf

PORTRAITS OF POTTERS BAR

People, places and incidents before, during and after WWII

AUSTIN MACAULEY PUBLISHERS™
LONDON * CAMBRIDGE * NEW YORK * SHARJAH

Copyright © Aly Sharaf 2023

The right of Aly Sharaf to be identified as author of this work has been asserted by the author in accordance with sections 77 and 78 of the Copyright, Designs and Patents Act 1988.

All rights reserved. No part of this publication may be reproduced, stored in a retrieval system, or transmitted in any form or by any means, electronic, mechanical, photocopying, recording, or otherwise, without the prior permission of the publishers.

Any person who commits any unauthorised act in relation to this publication may be liable to criminal prosecution and civil claims for damages.

This is a work of fiction. Names, characters, businesses, places, events, locales, and incidents are either the products of the author's imagination or used in a fictitious manner. Any resemblance to actual persons, living or dead, or actual events is purely coincidental.

A CIP catalogue record for this title is available from the British Library.

ISBN 9781398486928 (Paperback)
ISBN 9781398486935 (ePub e-book)

www.austinmacauley.com

First Published 2023
Austin Macauley Publishers Ltd®
1 Canada Square
Canary Wharf
London
E14 5AA

Table of Contents

Map	11
Introduction	12
Run, Adolf, Run	14
Deskmate	18
The Girl Who Walked from Warrengate Farm	20
Three Wartime Heroes	22
The Rev Aubrey Argyll, DD	27
Chrewdless the Cruel Hairdresser	31
The Abdication	35
The Fire Hydrant	37
The Knitting Episode	40
The Persecution of Ig	43
Mr Magnus	46
The Fair	53
New Tel Aviv	58
Juanita and the Waxworks	62
Fujihito Matsumori	64
Rationing	67
The Tracks	71
I Don't Want to Set the World on Fire	76

Der Old Vic	79
Field Day	82
Gas	85
Sandbags or Money Bags?	87
Evacuees	89
Natushka	93
The Cloudburst	94
The Edith Duckett Story	97
Diana Garrod	99
Easter	103
Napsbury	106
Mr Spink	110
Dr Mary Allen	112
A Matter of Course	115
Arnhem Armada	118
The King's Stammer	121
Singing in the Shelters	123
Sleeping in the Shelters	126
Card-carrying Colonists	131
How not to Earn Five Bob	133
Primrose	136
Pivotal Point	138
Bags	142
Riding Down from Bangor	147
Holidays at Home	151
Omar Khayyam	155
WASPS, where is Your Sting?	157

Faith, Hope and Verity	**159**
Wireless Icons	**161**
Moscow Dynamos	**164**
The Guard's Chapel	**166**
Christmas	**168**
Dormitory Town?	**175**
Postscript	**178**
E = MC – What?	**179**
Don't Slate the Slate	**180**
Deskmates	**182**
Dancing in the Streets	**185**
Thomas Freshwater Briggs, 1858–1948	**187**
Postscript	**190**
Charles and Mary Lamb	**191**
The Sweetest Soul	**195**

Map

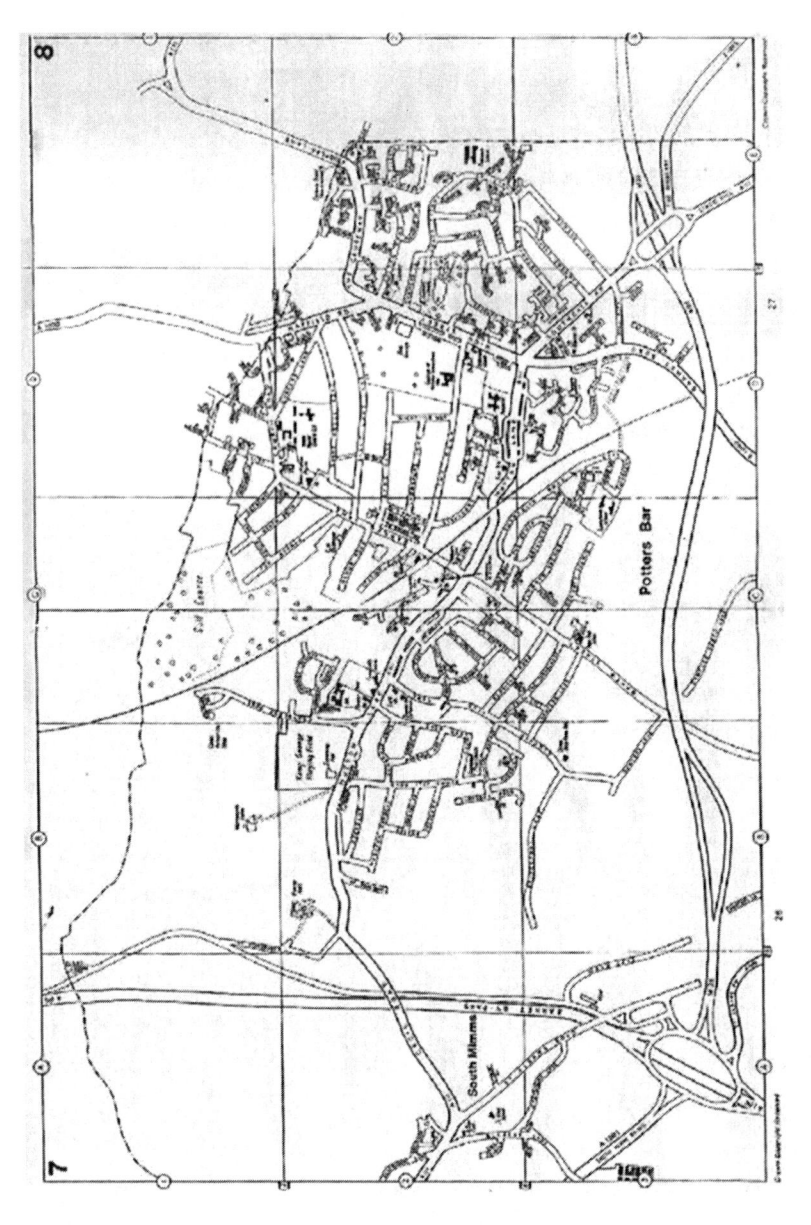

Introduction

Is an introduction really necessary? Frankly I don't think so; it seems to me that the following pages speak quite adequately for themselves. Yet perhaps I do owe prospective readers some explanation of why this book came into being.

As the title shows, it has two main subjects: WWII and Potters Bar – which is my hometown, almost but not quite a suburb of London. Interest in WWII, which ended more than sixty years ago, far from diminishing, is constantly on the increase. Nearly every week a book appears dealing with this or that aspect of the conflict; the global public already has extensive knowledge of it, yet hungers for more. The same cannot be said of Potters Bar. Outside Britain, there are probably no more than a few thousand people who have even heard of it. But for me it was the hub of the universe as I grew up – passing through childhood, then adolescence, eventually teetering on the brink of adulthood. And that whole process took place against the backdrop of the war: the years leading up to it (when it was germinating, so to speak) – those of its actual duration – and then those of its aftermath. All these periods affected me profoundly – and so did that beloved quasi-suburban home of mine where I lived through them all. Though I left it in the early fifties, to spend the rest of my life abroad, mostly in the Middle East, its influence remains, ineradicable. Thus those two subjects – home and war – were and still are for me inextricably linked. Like the war, the hometown represents the past. Revisiting the one – as I have in effect done in writing this book – meant reliving the other.

My memories of both are still extremely vivid – albeit many of them a child's eye view. As I was jotting them down, at first just for my own satisfaction, it occurred to me: why shouldn't I add my recollections to those others already in the bookshops – there might well be quite a lot in them to interest twenty-first-century readers. 'People, places and incidents' they'd otherwise never hear of. Not just battles and air-raids, victories and defeats – the hard stuff of war – all that's common knowledge. But – the things we did against that ever-present background. At home, at school, as we started out in jobs. Falling in love – and out of it! In short, the way we lived our everyday lives and yes, in spite of continuous tragic realities, the fun we had – tremendous fun at times. Read all about it!

None of this is fiction. All these pieces depict either my own personal experience or that of people close to me; a few of their accounts take us back to WWI – quite recent past in the '30s and '40s. Some of this material is now known only to me; unless I record it, when I pass on, it will be known to no one; it will be lost forever. As mentioned in the entry called 'The Edith Duckett Story', John Steinbeck had just such a realisation about things his father had told him, and acted accordingly.

I didn't keep diaries. I've always had an exceptionally good memory and I've relied on that. It's still above average but I know that may not always be the case. As the (very) senior citizen I have become, I have to ensure that so-called "senior moments" don't encroach and steal away those treasured recollections beyond recall. Therefore, better get them all on record while I still can. Hence this book.

I think that will do by way of "Introduction". So now I will step aside and indeed let these pages speak for themselves.

Run, Adolf, Run

It was 1938. Coming home from Sunday school one afternoon – I used to walk a good mile there and back – I passed by the main Potters Bar cemetery in Mutton Lane. And who should I see standing guard outside but an SS trooper, complete with swastika armband. And this wasn't fancy dress, à la Prince Harry, but the real thing. It was therefore by no means an ordinary moment in the history of my hometown's principal burial ground. Because at that very instant, who should be behind its lych gate, performing an ambassadorial duty, but Herr von Ribbentrop, Hitler's then man in London. Paying his respects to the twenty-two-man crew of the Zeppelin that, in WWI, bent on bombing England, had crashed in nearby Cuffley. Their remains had been brought for interment to Potters Bar, the nearest site available. I have no doubt that nowadays Cuffley, then virtually a suburb of Potters Bar, is self-sufficient in cemeteries as in everything else. But in 1918, when that famous crash happened, it was only a mere outpost. Like South Mimms had been for centuries, till the M25, from which it is a major exit, catapulted it into prominence. So that it has now outgrown its parent "city", and become the tail that wags the dog.

Precocious brat that I was in 1938, sole child in a household of several adults, I'd been listening assiduously to the radio (the wireless as we called it then) plus reading the papers, like the grown-ups. So I was well briefed about the scheduled ambassadorial visit. But my interpretation of what I saw was far from adult. In my eight-year-old gullibility I'd thought that this soldier standing guard was actually Ribbentrop himself. I went on believing that for quite a while. To the extent that I would tell people: 'The first famous person I ever saw was Herr von Ribbentrop'. Eventually, I had to retract this and admit that the first celebs I did indeed clap eyes on, a mere stone's throw away in the High Street, were none other than Jack Hulbert and Cicely Courtneidge, a well-known husband-and-wife theatrical team, performing a public function – opening a furniture store to be precise. A somewhat more prosaic assignment than that of the Nazi envoy.

No doubt the SS man standing guard in our lane was suitably equipped to deal with any hostile demonstration that might have broken out. But in fact none did. Indeed, apart from officials, hardly anyone had turned up to watch the proceedings, let alone demonstrate against them and, except for myself, there were barely even any casual passers-by. Von Ribbentrop had hardly taken Potters Bar by storm.

Nevertheless, he and his junta were quite soon to make their impact on our native heath. Their Zeppelin might have missed its mark in 1918 but, a generation later, the Luftwaffe, with its bombs and land mines, plus Werner von Braun's infamous V1s and V2s (pilotless planes and rockets) claimed their victims among our citizens. The names of civilians who perished in WWII are not inscribed on either of the town's two war memorials. But I know them all – seven children and four adults. There were Ada and Ida, two maiden sisters well-known by sight to us as they often waited at the bus-stop opposite our house. They were killed in a direct hit on their home in Laurel Avenue, the street running between Mutton Lane and the main north-south railway line. Then there were the little Burgoyne children, their grandfather a crony of my own granddad at the Bowling Club; they were fast asleep at his home on the High Street when a fatal air raid happened. There was, too, the Walsh family – my stepfather's colleague lost his wife and all their five children to the V2 rocket, launched from Peenemunde in Holland, as the war entered its final stages. Germany was at bay. Von Braun boasted of his "achievement" in the Hollywood saga obscenely entitled *I reach for the stars*. Lastly, there was Mr Deale, whose daughter Rosemary, a schoolmate of mine, had died aged eight of a kidney disease – a tragedy that shook the whole of our school, Cranborne. Her resting place and that of her baby sister Iris lies between those of my grandparents and the Zeppelin crew – their father was among many killed in an attack on Kings Cross, the central London terminus for north-east bound trains. So, our town was indubitably on the front line, situated on that railway line as well as on the Great North Road, alias the A1000, a twin north-south artery.

When landmines fell on the cemetery itself there were no casualties but the desecration was enough to make people 'glut their ire' in a big way, hurling clods at the German graves in a frenzied outburst of hatred and far-from-forgiveness. Pacificism had a very low profile in Potters Bar that day. More than half a century later, feelings are so different: 'It's all over. It was such a long time ago. Like the Napoleonic wars – history'. But way back then, it wasn't history. It was today.

The Zeppelin demands some elaboration. Everyone knew about it though, like the Titanic and Captain Scott's exploits in Antarctica, it happened well before 'media' covered, and over-covered, everything. Before wireless, let alone TV. But there was the press; the public was well informed. Constantly urged: *Read all about it! Star, News and Standard!* (The main evening papers). And they certainly did.

In the thirties, as I was growing up, people were still very much aware of WWI. After all, it wasn't all that long before – a mere couple of decades. So many men had fought in it – millions had died and millions more were maimed and/or shell-shocked. And so many millions bereaved. Women like Ida and Ada lost their fiancés, never to be replaced.

I suppose it's been like that since war began. Since before Homer's time and ever since.

The Zeppelin provided an incident that the imagination latched on to. It also put Cuffley on the map, making it if not exactly a household name at least not an unfamiliar one. And for some there was a more personal memory. One of our friends told us how, as she was giving birth in North London in 1918, she looked out of the clinic window and saw the Zeppelin going down in flames. Fresh as it still was in the national memory in 1939, when our state of war with Germany was declared, it was widely expected that Hitler would use Zeppelins. But he didn't. Like gas. *Deo gratias*. The weaponry he chose was quite different – albeit lethal too.

In fact WWII was largely expected to be a repetition, a continuation – a sequel, if you will – of that earlier conflict. But it wasn't. It was a WW in its own right – with its own specific horrors.

***

While on the subject of Von Ribbentrop, I cannot omit a final note. One of the top hits of the early '40s was a parody of *Run, Rabbit, Run!* It went like this:

Run, Adolf, run Adolf, run, run, run!
Look what you've been gone and done, done, done.
We will knock the stuffing out of you,
Field Marshal Goering and Goebbels too.
You've lost your place in the sun, sun, sun.

We've got the men, and the mon, mon, mon.
You will flop, with Herr von Ribbentrop.
So run Adolf, run Adolf, run, run, run!

Deskmate

At Cranborne School, in 'the second class of the infants', we were presided over by a teacher appropriately named Miss English. She was a very pretty woman and it was a lovely classroom. Bright and airy, the walls adorned by a series of scenes from Hans Christian Andersen. Featuring, especially, trolls. I had never before heard of these creatures; I found them fascinating. Were there trolls perhaps in our countryside too? Maybe Granddad and I might bump into some of them on our long country walks. These had already become an institution of ours when I was only four years old.

Few fellow Cranbornians have left a more vivid or lasting impression on me than my deskmate of that year, Roger Limbrey. Though we went through all six classes of the school together, it was in 'the second class of the infants' that we were at our closest. Sharing the desk as we did, we seized the chance to have a good look at each other's genitals – an aspect of education, after all. Especially, when kids don't have siblings of the opposite sex at home – young ones, with their baths and nappy changes – there's bound to be a gap in knowledge about that usually carefully covered up area. Who can blame youngsters like us for trying to find out more? So under the benign gaze of the trolls (though not of Miss English) we satisfied our curiosity and, once satisfied, moved on to other things – other sources of interest or amusement. Like, even, our lessons – which weren't entirely devoid of entertainment or fun.

I guess it wasn't only Roger and I who indulged in that illicit though entirely natural activity; perhaps it's the norm at that age. I reckon it fizzles out after mid-infants. A 'been there, done that' attitude sets in – you've become a bit more grown up and a shade blasé along with it.

However that may be, it can't be denied that, one way or another, you get to feel close to long-term deskmates. You can't help but care about them. I was particularly concerned about Roger because he had to walk a very long way to school and back – much of his route going along the path that parallels the railway between the stations of Potters Bar and Brookmans Park the next one to the north. His home was situated in the, for me, remote and unchartered territory beyond the point where this path ends. Giving way to a minor road; here the Brookmans Park catchment area begins. (Why didn't he go to school there, then? Perhaps it would have been even more difficult of access). This minor road weaves between such isolated villages and hamlets as Swanley Bar, ever synonymous for me with the back of beyond – how far off the beaten track can you get? Mind you, we're talking here of some sixty years ago – perhaps these hamlets have become megalopolises by now. But that's how they were when Roger went to school. When at last on his long trudge home he sighted his front door, wouldn't he be feeling utterly exhausted, more than ready for bed? Especially, as he'd have to get up very early next morning to tackle the outward traipse. Fortunately, we weren't given homework at Cranborne infants but if we had been he'd have been expected to do it just like any child living next door to the school.

Yes, I felt really concerned about Roger. But I never heard him complain. Perhaps he actually enjoyed his exacting schedule! Moreover, it didn't seem to do him any harm. Maybe, on the contrary, it toughened him up – at any rate, he went through all six of the Cranborne classes with aplomb, featuring in school photo after school photo, his health apparently quite unimpaired.

The Girl Who Walked from Warrengate Farm

Roger wasn't the only one forced to rely a lot on Shanks's pony. Most people walked to work. Quite long distances sometimes. A few cycled. No one used cars, their own or others'; in fact, very few people had them. A taxi was practically an unknown sight on the streets of Potters Bar – though there was always one parked by the railway station.

There was a girl who used to walk every day from Warrengate Farm, way out in the countryside near North Mimms; she would go past our house and continue up Mutton Lane. Presumably she was going home; I never saw her going in the opposite direction – maybe she did that when I was asleep or at school.

I sensed there was some sort of secret about her, something taboo, unmentionable. When she suddenly died it was rumoured she had committed suicide. Another taboo – were they connected? She provided one of several thought-provoking rectangles there in the township's quickly filling up cemetery. Looking back, I can only put two and two together – had she got pregnant and taken an obvious escape route? Things were far from permissive in England those days.

Pregnancy wasn't the only situation that prompted folk to end it all. And not only women did that. Moreover, it wasn't exclusively the lot of those tarnished by rumour. "Respectable" people resorted to it, women and men alike. Dr Porter, for instance – stalwart provider of 'laughing gas' anaesthesia at the dentist's. And Ronald Clefane. He and his wife Evelyn ranked high among my mother's many glamorous friends. Very attractive – in the style of the thirties' cinema greats, epitomised by William Powell and Myrna Loy, Clark Gable, Robert Donat, Ronald Coleman. A style that flourished then and then only, never before or after. The Clefanes had exactly that look. Our own local Ronald 'had it all', 'such a lot going for him.' Why ever should he want to quit? And Dr Porter?

Putting two and two together again, I can only assume that they knew they had cancer and weren't prepared to let it do it its way. So they made their brave exits.

Three Wartime Heroes

1. **Pierre Roche**
2. **Mr Bath**
3. **Pat Garland**

Pierre Roche

We had a French neighbour whom I'll call Pierre Roche. His English wife, I'll call her Maggie. They lived at that pivotal point which, I've worked out from the map (qv), was the absolute centre of Potters Bar, where the N-S, E-W lines bisect each other. Odd that foreigners should be living there – England was very far from being "multicultural" those days.

Les Rochè shared their home with Maggie's sister and her family; they had a little girl called Claudette; another, named Odile, had died some years earlier and was laid to rest in that part of the cemetery set aside for children. The sadness of that place smote me even then; I wasn't entirely heartless, spoilt brat though I undoubtedly was.

I felt a certain pride and possessiveness, sitting next to Pierre across the aisle on the No. 29 bus. On leave from the Maginot Line, his French Army uniform contrasting starkly with that of the SS guard chaperoning von Ribbentrop. No swastikas here!

Maggie was a close friend of my mother. She was in our home, listening to the news, that day in June 1940 when the fall of France was announced – by Alvar Liddell and Bruce Belfrage, leading anchors of wartime wireless.

The years of conflict went their inexorable way. Pierre fought in the Resistance. Maggie remained in England – and entered into another relationship. (She also narrowly escaped being murdered by a serial killer operating in the area, whose tactics included submersing victims' bodies in acid). She confessed to my mother,

'I can't resist men, I can't help it! I'm irresistibly drawn to them!'

Thus I learned, quite early in my life: 'Some women are like that. Amply oversexed. It's not their fault. They're just made that way.'

Pierre eventually lost his life in the Resistance and Maggie made another confession,

'He haunts me.'

In horror I imagined him appearing to her in their Mutton Lane bedroom, leaving her to be tortured by her conscience. It was especially hard for her when she had to go to France to collect his posthumously awarded Croix de Guerre.

I had reason, didn't I, to feel proud sitting next to him on the bus?

Mr Bath

Mr Bath was one of the most memorable of our teachers. Not least because he was a 'conchy' – conscientious objector. It was the first year of the war, 1939–1940. The confusing, seemingly unreal months of the 'phoney war' petered out and the Blitz began. Nothing phoney, or unreal, about that! Once, in late 1940, we stayed up all night, having breakfast (fried tomatoes, I well recall) in the early hours. From Potters Bar looking due south we could see the night sky lit up as London burned. As we saw in the morning papers what an achievement, that they were produced at all and distributed as usual despite that inferno – St Paul's was at the very heart of the conflagration.

Not surprisingly, Brits as a whole didn't take kindly to those who didn't want to hit back. People like Mr Bath. Not surprisingly too, he'd received his share of white feathers, symbolic accusations of cowardice sent anonymously and hardly courageously – through the post or shoved, sometimes with shit through letter boxes. Exempted from the army, he was allowed to teach, that being seen as an acceptable alternative form of war service. Like ambulance driving, or working on the land. But it didn't impress everyone. Dressed in civvies, it took guts on his part to walk down the street flanked by his wife and baby, while other men had had to leave their dear ones behind to go half way across the world to fight and maybe die. It took guts – a different kind from what's required on, say, the Maginot Lane, but guts all the same. And Mr Bath had plenty of that.

He was no softie. In fact he was quite a stern disciplinarian. He had to be, to control kids like us. Once he made an example of me, together with my greatest friend, another Rosemary (surnamed Randall, and I also called her Roya) forcing us to stand in front of the class as punishment for some peccadillo – "talking", most probably, the cardinal classroom sin, of which we were often guilty. We certainly didn't make his already difficult life one little bit easier, no denying it!

But there was another side to Mr Bath as far as I was concerned. I was in love with him. And my main dread was that people would find out. This could easily happen because of my proneness to blushing. Prone then and I still am – though nowadays, mercifully, I have nothing to blush about. Nothing to be ashamed or embarrassed about, like secret loves or not having done my homework. Now, my conscience and my heart are delightfully free. Then, it was a very different matter. To what ridicule might I not be exposed if People Found Out? I had to have a strategy ready for instant use, as certain things might suddenly trigger the blush. One of these was a song, very popular then – there was as yet no such thing as 'top of the pops' but that was what it amounted to. It went like this:

An apple for the teacher
Will always do the trick
When you can't do your lessons in
Arithmetic

Should this burst forth on the wireless while we were having lunch (dinner, as we always called it), tea or breakfast or supper, I'd suddenly go scarlet to the roots of my hair. I had to dash instantly for cover – the loo was the nearest available, my place at the table just by the door facilitating such speedy retreats.

I don't think anyone ever did rumble my secret – or the ruse designed to cover it up. Anyway, in a mercifully short while I got over that particular infatuation.

Pat Garland

People may or may not have suspected another such – a much more serious one. A genuine love, in fact. The focus of this was Pat Garland. Now there was a war hero of the really front-line calibre. None more so, even his VC brother Donald who, at the age of 21, crashed his plane on the advancing German army in France. Like a kamikaze or indeed a suicide bomber, and truly a martyr if ever there was one.

There were four Garland brothers and all of them died in the war. Three were in the RAF – Pat and Donald as well as Desmond who flew on bombing raids over enemy territory, was shot down and also granted a high award posthumously. Their mother had to go to Buckingham Palace to receive their honours; when asked about her feelings she spoke briefly but movingly about her grief and her pride. They are all commemorated in the RAF church at St. Clement Danes in the Strand. The fourth brother, Jack, was a doctor; he too passed away in wartime but not in combat.

During his lifetime Pat was a legend in our family. He and his wife Molly were a glamorous duo indeed – again mirroring the movie icons of the times – Myrna Loy, William Powell *et al*. Pat joked about 'Molly's little acorns' and their life together which we could not but picture as the acme of sheer romance. 'Little acorns' didn't stop her being a superwoman. In those times you didn't have to have big boobs to be a big star – all you needed was star quality.

Another of Pat's memorable statements was how he'd threatened to beat up some people in a cinema who had failed to stand up for the national anthem – 'God Save the King' – which it was de rigueur those days to play at the end of every show.

Dashing, dare-devil, devil-may-care – that was Pat. It went without saying, he was spectacularly handsome too. A close friend of my Uncle Sid, also in the RAF, who like all his siblings – my mother and aunts Doris and Elsie – attracted wonderfully charismatic friends. (Another of these was Jack Hawkins, a schoolmate of Sid's; as teenagers they did amateur theatricals together including Gilbert and Sullivan; Hawkins went on to become a film actor, very outstanding, notably in *Bridge on the River Kwai*.)

I was aged about eight when Pat entered my life. I was utterly entranced by him. And this too I didn't want broadcast from the rooftops – I hugged it to myself. Although it was my nature to be timid, I simply couldn't be when Pat was around. One day I boldly addressed him,

'Would you please kiss me?'

I wasn't in the least surprised by my boldness; in his presence it had seemed perfectly logical and natural. And at once he bent down from his great height to grant my wish.

And he also submitted a request that was granted – his great height was involved in that too. Because of it he had been debarred from flying. But he wanted to avenge Donald, and so wrote to King George-VI asking him to overrule the ban; the King at once agreed. Ironically, Pat's height was the reason he didn't survive the crash that eventually happened, seated as he was in the low-roofed cockpit.

It so chanced that around this time I had to go to the dentist for an extraction. Those days it was the practice for 'laughing gas' to be used as anaesthesia. I'd heard how patients babbled under this, giving away their innermost secrets. I was so afraid I might "reveal all" about Pat – the intense adoration I felt for him but so far kept strictly to myself. I'd so ardently hoped no one had any inkling of it – how he was dominating my every thought.

My mother, seeing how nervous I was and eager to hearten me, declared, 'Don't worry! Just think about Pat!'

The Rev Aubrey Argyll, DD

We used to go to the Baptist Church on the Great North Road. You're almost out of town once you reach there, going towards Barnet, and the monument to the battle there in 1475 where Warwick the Kingmaker met his Waterloo, so to speak, and where the Martians landed in HG Wells's 'War of the Worlds.' The Baptist Church…Probably my mother decided on this as the best solution to my christening problem. I hadn't been baptised at the usual age, about six months, because she was hospitalised then for an indefinite period. No doubt the family – Granddad, Granny, my aunts Elsie and Doris, who had all taken me to their bosom, caring for me in every way, had no doubt thought it preferable to wait for Mother's release rather than holding a ceremony without her. But that release didn't happen till I was four years old – in fact, on my fourth birthday exactly; the date must have been chosen on purpose.

I well recall the reunion – with one whom I saw as a glamorous and interesting guest rather than a long-lost parent. Probably we had not seen each other since I was three months old when she was placed in the hospital. I don't know whether I was ever taken to visit her there; in all likelihood children's visits were not allowed, since it was a mental hospital. The condition she was suffering from was a post-puerperal one – caused by my birth – and at the time of its onset there was little hope of recovery. No doubt it is far better understood, and treated, nowadays than it was in the 1930s. Even then, hers was considered an unusual case; she told me it had been written up in one of the professional journals; I suppose I could have gone searching for it and learned many facts, but as I was sure these would make painful reading, I let well alone.

My first words to Mother on our reunion were, 'I've fallen in the arabus' – a word I knew then, aged four, but subsequently forgot. It's not to be found in every dictionary. Though, as is often the case, Chambers provides an exception. I'd learned it from Granddad – you could say he gave me a university education before I went to school – I was familiar with the names of all the numerous flowers and shrubs he planted, duly marking their plots with a lovingly inscribed peg along with their seed packets.

'Fallen in the arabus.' Mother reminded me of this, the first sentence I ever addressed to her (assuming I'd not been to see her in hospital) when I visited her in 1956 – another reunion, after my move to Egypt on marriage in 1952. 'Well,' she added, 'you've fallen in it now, all right.'

Mother had missed out on me and I had missed out on her. Granny and Granddad, Doris and Elsie, had brought me up through those supremely formative years, teaching me everything I knew including whatever knowledge I had of the English language – no mean mastery if 'arabus' is anything to go by.

So I was four and perhaps it was thought that the usual christening ceremony would be inappropriate. Probably it was Mother who put forward the idea – better to wait yet again – this time for the adult rituals that are provided by the Baptist Church, thereby allowing me to make my own decision about whether or not to enter Christianity. She must have made a point of discussing this with the then minister at the church, the Rev Aubrey Argyll, DD An outstanding personality. A young man and strikingly good-looking, married with one child; these very human aspects charmingly offset his intellectual aura.

My clearest memory of him is connected with another birthday of mine, "arguably" my best ever – my ninth, in June 1939. War clouds were already closely amassing, but that didn't stop us having fun, and the Rev. Argyll joined in it wholeheartedly. Sitting with others on our stairs, the auditorium of my makeshift theatre. I was putting on a show, written and produced by me and of course I starred in it too, my best friends allocated supporting roles. Can't recall a thing now of what it was about, but the mechanics of its staging remain vivid.

301 Mutton Lane, Potters Bar, Middlesex[*] might have been purpose-built for home theatricals. The hall was the stage, the downstairs bedroom and the bathroom/loo the wings, while the stairs seated the audience. So our eminent guest sat there, mucking in joyfully with everyone else. He'd brought me a very nice present – Winnie the Pooh. It was all so idyllic, even down to the strawberries and cream tea laid on in the garden: a really Wimbledon air about that, as Mummy had installed on the lawn a device called a 'Kumbak' for practising tennis. She was '*une grande sportive*', tennis and swimming being her

---

[*] It was in Middesex throughout my entire residence there. Later a flick of a bureaucrat's pen transferred it to Hertfordshire

favourites and she excelled at both. I didn't share either her interest or her talent for sport – in fact I was quite the opposite. "Head always stuck in a book" as an acquaintance of those days summed me up.

There was a tennis court near the Baptist Church and Mummy made good use of it. In fact the church was a strong focus of social as well as religious life. For me as well as Mum. There was the Sunday school with its activities including outings to, among other places, the seaside and parkland called 'California in England.' My grandmother came with me on one of these trips and so did Marion, my next-door neighbour, and dear friend, a year my junior. Then – most fun of all, the songs. They were hymns really but hymns with a difference – lively and jolly, ideal for community singing. Hardly Hot Gospel but top of my pops was:

Wide, wide as the ocean,
High as the heavens above,
Deep, deep as the deepest sea
Is my Saviour's love.

I, oh so unworthy,
Still am a child of His care
For His word teaches me that His love reaches me
Everywhere!

What a thrill we got, belting that out of a Sunday. You didn't have to be a practising or even a believing Christian to relish it thoroughly. (Doesn't Richard Dawkins today confess to enjoying carol singing?) And I was really delighted, decades later, when I heard my own children similarly belting it out at Clergy House primary school in Khartoum. It was quite broad-minded, was it not, of my then spouse, Muslim that he was, to let them attend such a non-Muslim establishment.

My joining the Sunday school was the occasion for my receiving what was, and still is, one of my most precious possessions. An illustrated Bible (King James's version) especially appealing to children, with marvellous – and anonymous – portrayals of Old and New Testament scenes. Mummy must have shopped around carefully to choose it. All of these pictures are an inspiration, particularly the one of the Virgin Mary and St Joseph, with the infant Christ, receiving the shepherds – to this day it gives me joy and comfort. At the end of the Book are several maps showing the background to the Bible story; Egypt, Alexandria and the northern part what is now Saudi Arabia. Libya and Cyrenaica too, illustrating St Paul's journey. All this seems to me uncannily to foretell my eventually coming to rest, as it were, in the Middle East, the Arab world. Like 'I've fallen in the arabus' – among several pointers to the place I was destined to go, and remain for the greater part of my life. All unbeknownst to us all at 301 Mutton Lane in the nineteen-thirties.

Mummy must have been very sorry indeed when the Rev Argyll was transferred from Potter Bar. Perhaps that explains why she looks so upset in a seaside snap taken in August 1939. Or perhaps it was simply the immanence of war. We'd been on holiday in Kent and came home on Friday, 1st September. Crossing London from one terminus to another (Victoria to Kings Cross) Mummy said to me, 'You'll be able to say you went along Whitehall the day before war was declared.' Hitler had just attacked Poland which Britain was pledged to defend. Actually Mr Chamberlain didn't make the declaration till Sunday, the 3rd, at 11 am. Reluctantly, I interrupted a 'playgame', a favourite activity I shared with Marion, to listen to that. Clutching our gas masks as the air-raid warnings terrifyingly wailed. Millions thought, *Gosh, he hasn't lost much time!" Panic! But, Deo gratias, it was a false alarm. And we proceeded to get on with our 'playgame', and our lives, as best we could.*

Chrewdless the Cruel Hairdresser

There were many delightful spinoffs to Mother's return from her exile in hospital. For me, perhaps the most enjoyable was the routine she and I soon established of my pretending to be her hairdresser. After a morning packed with household chores – cooking, shopping, washing up and the like – she would relax in the afternoon. Settling with her knitting (she was a champion knitter) and her favourite magazine the Nursing Mirror or a book from Boots the Chemist: that nation-wide pharmacy giant lured extra customers by its very well-stocked library. Mummy would knit and read simultaneously while I messed about with her hair.

No ordinary hairdressing this; it wasn't just a matter of combing and plaiting and setting and shampooing. It was an imaginary posh salon whose staff included one Chewdless, notorious for her cruel treatment of customers. They would plead to be spared her attention and beg for 'some other assistant – please!' But the answer usually was, 'Sorry, only Chewdless is available now.' So they just had to grin and bear it, with frequent exclamations of 'Ouch!' Mummy and I went along with all this, just like Marion and me with our playgames.

In the meantime Granddad would treat himself to his daily unwinding ritual, namely 'forty winks'. It was partly this that enabled him to live the busy life he did. A routine, and a conviction, that he shared with Mr Churchill whose image, giving the V-for-victory sign from the steps of No. 10, beamed down on us benignly from atop our wireless set, throughout the dark war years. Like in most Brit homes – millions and millions of them. A notable exception was, however, the case of Philip Larkin. Front-runner for the job of Poet Laureate, to succeed John Betjeman, Larkin's mantelpiece boasted photos of none other than Adolf Hitler. As for Betjeman, his infamous invitation to 'Come friendly bombs and fall on Slough' should surely have disqualified him instantly for the royally bestowed sinecure. I should have thought that one of the prime requisites, the *sine qua non* in fact for laureateship, would be a simple love of one's country –

no need for fanatical jingoism but just the natural feeling most people have for their native place. 'Breathes there the man with soul so dead…' That both these top poets, the incumbent and the frontrunner, lacked such basic feelings – and no one apparently minded! – astonishes me.

But back to Chewdless. Granddad's afternoon nap along with Mummy's and my, hairdressing exercise, were also presided over not only by Mr Churchill but by another national institution, to wit the Big Bands, on the wireless. These were the UK's answer to Glen Miller and his like across the Atlantic. Foremost among our maestros was Henry Hall. His vastly popular music would accompany my – or rather Chewdless's – grim antics with comb and scissors. She specialised in pulling the clients' hair and making of it such tangles Hercules might have balked at unravelling. Gordian knots indeed! As for her shampoo-and-set, it was nothing short of a torture session. (I didn't actually hurt Mummy while performing this drama; it was just acting pure and simple). This was a new kind of fun experience for her; surely she hadn't had anything like that in the hospital. And it was part, no doubt, of her getting-to-know-me process; after all, she'd had no hand in bringing me up till I was four and famously 'fell in the arabus'.

Chewdless the Cruel Hairdresser was one of several fictitious characters with whom I populated my only-child solitude. She was second only to Bimby, imaginary friend par excellence, and way ahead of Mini Mauri (the baddy) and Dan and Gloria (the good guys) in the ever-ongoing play-games with Marion. Yes, they were as ongoing as any soap you may care to mention.

The Chewdless antics took place against a backdrop – scenery you might call it, or props – in the form of carvings on the sideboards that were part of our living-room furniture. Old fashioned stuff this – hardly IKEA! These carvings, for me, represented far distant cities, continents and oceans, so I wasn't exactly lying when I told schoolmates, 'We have the sea in our house.' Not surprisingly, that caused some raised eyebrows. What further proof was needed that 'Iris Briggs is a first-rate little liar if ever there was one.'

Mummy had her knitting patterns propped up against these props, as Henry Hall charmed the afternoon away with his programme of pop songs. Starting and finishing with his signature tune:

Here's to the next time'
And a merry meeting
Here's to the next time

We send you all our greeting,
Set it to music
Sing it in rhyme
Now, all together;
"Here's to next time!"

And in between the start and finish were plenty of numbers sung by Brian Lawrence, his vocalist – 'crooner' was the term in use those days, the archetype being Bing Crosby. Brian Lawrence must have packed a load of sex appeal into his voice – no TV to rely on then. He had masses of fans countrywide. Mummy and one of her naughtier friends (they were all pretty naughty, for that matter, and unconventional) Evelyn Clefane, nurtured a yen to meet up with him. I heard them discussing this; I'm not sure how far they got with it. Whether just writing to him or actually fixing a meeting. Neither outcome would surprise me as I seem to have inherited a tendency towards such goings on – witness my writing, many years later, in collaboration with a friend whom I'll call Madge Smythe, to the comedian Vic Oliver. And also with Madge, actually pulling off a meeting with one of her idols, namely the 'father of all Wagnerian tenors', Set Svanholm, who often partnered Kirsten Flagstad (possibly greatest of all Wagnerian sopranos). Madge was the most ardent Wagner buff I've ever met and thought nothing of queueing all night to see such star performers. Mr Svanholm was kind enough to respond positively to our approach, inviting us to tea at the Walfdorf Hotel – all perfectly respectable, I must stress! – and regaling us with charming anecdotes about Flagstad. An event to remember all our lives, and to commemorate it I bought Madge a bunch of violets – I hope she kept it forever! I don't know, because we regrettably lost touch.

She too had memories of those Henry Hall afternoons. Being a few years younger than me, she was a mere toddler at the Chewdless time and had pronounced the band leader's name 'Enjaw'. From which she'd derived a motto, 'Enjaw yourself!'

I must put on record, of all the British Big Bands flourishing in the '30s, 'Enjaw', superb as he was, wasn't my favourite. That had to be Geraldo, principally because of his top vocalist Dorothy Carless. I really admired that woman. I could tell from the snippets of talk with her inserted into the show that she was a real intellectual. Albeit a 'crooner'. No oxymoron there.

So, when Mr Sims our headmaster inevitably asked Mummy what did I want to be when I grew up, and she answered, with some embarrassment, 'A crooner, I'm afraid', they needn't have worried, either of them. Being a crooner doesn't rule out being a PhD – or vice versa.

The Abdication

It was January 1935. We were standing at the top of the stairs, between our bedroom (Mummy's shared with me) and Doris's. Two completely different ambiences. I could write reams about Doris's lovely sanctum and how it reflected her lovely self, with its exquisitely delicate décor, full of beautiful and finely made objects. So poignantly virginal. It radiated her purity and sheer goodness, her devotion to duty – perhaps the most striking of her many fine qualities. She deserved every bit of it, she'd more than earned that 'lovely sanctum'. Our room was very ordinary in comparison – but beloved all the same.

From that vantage point, the little landing, the highest place in the house, the wonderful portrait of my grandmother looked down – she who perhaps more than any other (though they all played very substantial roles) brought me up, my much more than 'mother surrogate'. And it is no coincidence, I think, that her grandmother (whose name I don't so far know, though I hope one day to find out) brought her up, her own mother being for reasons likewise so far unknown, *hors de combat* and, I think, out of the country too. She seems to have been one of those nineteenth-century Englishwomen who pursued their destiny abroad. Grandmother Florence Rodwell as a young woman, dressed in Edwardian or late Victorian fashion, looked down in marvellous blessing on our family home.

Mummy and Auntie, far taller than five-year-old me, were discussing over my head the "breaking news" – King George V had just died. That meant Edward VIII had already inherited the throne. But, as I was soon to learn, this wasn't simply a matter of one monarch succeeding another. As they had done for so many centuries in our country – since way back before the Conquest, since before Wyllyott's Manor nearby (the most interesting, and ancient building in Potters Bar, mentioned in Domesday Book) was built. Not a bit like King Edward VII taking over from Queen Victoria. No. There were other factors involved. Or rather there was one other factor. Its name was Mrs Simpson.

This was the topic destined to dominate conversation for many months to come, culminating in what I have to call the broadcast to end all broadcasts. Of course, we didn't have TV then, but we didn't need it. Sufficient unto the day are the media thereof – the wireless and the papers, the newsreels in cinemas, not to mention word of mouth – together those more than satisfied our need. And greed. We absolutely had to know everything about that celeb (although celebs as such hadn't yet been invented). She stared out at you wherever you looked. Mrs Simpson. And I couldn't for the life of me see what all the fuss was about. What was so special about her? She didn't strike me as being in the least pretty – like say my teacher Miss English or Molly Hargreaves, the girl next-door-but-two – a beauty fit for Hollywood. If he'd wanted to marry either of those it would have been quite understandable. But that woman looked so plain, so run-of-the-mill. So why on earth should he be so keen to make her his wife – and our queen? And why on earth should they the powers that were (I heard the words 'Government' and 'Prime Minister' such a lot those days, not quite sure what they meant) – why should they be so adamant he didn't? Little five-year-old me just couldn't grasp what it was all about.

Weeks passed. Months passed. Then – it came. That 'mother of all broadcasts' (with due acknowledgement to Saddam Hussein who introduced this phrase into the English language). Never have I heard or seen, in any sort of media, news more dramatic than that: not 9/11, nor yet Diana's death; not the assassination of Kennedy nor even man's walking on the moon.

The Abdication. The Abdication Speech. Its phrases resonate on and on through the nation's memory and our individual ones too. Undimmed by many a decade. The voice breaking with emotion, 'The woman I love!' And if that were possible – even more moving, 'God save the King!'

Shivers raced up and down my infant spine. Now I knew what it meant, all right – no one had to spell anything out for me. I understood – like I was the grownuppest of all grown-ups.

Yes – I was a precocious brat. I guess I still am!

The Fire Hydrant

It was 1937. I was leaning on our garden gate convalescing – after measles was it, or whooping cough? Watching the world go by. Watching it going along Mutton Lane. Especially watching my schoolmates and teachers, their daily stint performed, trudging homeward around 4 pm. I didn't pity them or gloat that I had had time off while they hadn't. On the contrary, I envied them – what had they been doing at Cranborne that I had missed out on? I didn't like skipping school. But there was an upside – in the morning, for instance, listening to the rag-and-bone man going his rounds with his distinctive, melancholy cry – which otherwise I never heard. But, more particularly, spending more time with Granddad – I could never get too much of that. He had a host of routine activities, self-allotted household tasks: to help my mother, who ran the show – Granny having been immobilised by a stroke – and Doris who was out all day at her office job in the City. I enjoyed watching him tackle his domestic chores. Incidentally, I never offered to help: it never occurred to me. Granddad didn't rebuke me; he seemed to accept: housework just wasn't my scene. Indeed he once remarked, 'Iris needs to be waited on hand and foot.' He had divined this fact about me when I was about seven or eight and didn't seem to mind.

    He had a highly efficient system for his work as secretary of the Bowling Club, a post he held for many years; I could surely have learned a thing or two of use to me in my future work – my job of a few years at Harrods Books and Library Department and, subsequently, my decades-long career with WHO in Egypt. Granddad generously gave secretarial services to the club for a very long time. 'He ought to be President!' I would protest. The incumbent of that position was one of the local big shots – unlike us, residing well and truly on the right side of the tracks; Granddad would regularly report to him at his posh house, sometimes taking me with him. Like that I got a feeling: here was an injustice – Granddad doing all the work, this guy getting all the kudos. In the end, though, things were rectified and he did indeed get the presidency, with Doris at his side as First Lady.

That 1937 afternoon, war was in the air. But not, as yet, our war. Nasty things were happening in other parts of the world. Firstly, there was the Spanish Civil War. Then there was the one going on between Japan and China; I realised we were supposed to be on China's side, though why, I couldn't fathom. Madame Chiang Kai Shek was the nearest we had to an "icon" those days; her pronouncements were always reported with great respect. The slogan 'Boycott Japanese goods' was very much in evidence – on the wireless, in the papers, and on posters in streets and shops. My main concern about this was that it might affect our supply of Christmas decorations, but I was reassured, 'Not to worry, we'll get them from Czechoslovakia.' Yes, and I could spell that, unlike most of my schoolmates or even plenty of adults. Also I had a very clear idea of where Japan and China were, not to mention Czechoslovakia and Spain. I was already a dab hand at geography, thanks of course to Granddad who had a special connection with it; he had spent his working life as a sorter in the post office and the addresses on the myriads of envelopes he handled intrigued him. He passed this fascination on to me, teaching me the capitals of the world well before I went to school. My favourite was Reykjavik – not many people, I discovered, had even heard of it. I could reel them off at the drop of a hat (and frequently did – no doubt to some folks' irritation) including those of the states of Australia: those haven't changed from that day to this but a lot of the others have, along with the countries they lorded it over. So that, now, we may not have to struggle to spell Czechoslovakia – only Czech Republic.

Granddad was "clever"; he had done very well at school; he loved learning and at one point had been offered the chance to go to university – very unusual among our class at that time, the late nineteenth century. But my great-grandfather hadn't agreed to this, believing it wouldn't be fair to his other sons.

Granddad could have been bitter about that but he wasn't. He loved teaching, albeit without benefit of college degrees. Above all, he loved teaching me. Perhaps he saw in me a promising recipient of all he had to transmit. Hence my boast, 'Granddad gave me a university education before I went to school.' Not far off the mark! I particularly recall his giving me a 'Learner's Dictionary' when I was quite little – people in their nineties could still learn from it. He made, too, a foray into French – what intrigued him more than any other word in that language was *dé* – thimble; and he commented, 'How interesting, a noun of only two letters.'

Whenever I leaned on our garden gate, lovingly inscribed 'Gathorne' after our former Wood Green home – and torn down, like our oak tree, by the new owners after we left – looking out at the passing-by world, always in the corner of my eye was a feature peculiar to 301. And that was – the Fire Hydrant. I've rarely come across this term, or had occasion to use it, except when it has cropped up once or twice in crosswords. The Fire Hydrant stood on the Verge. I'd grasped the fact that the Verge was outside our territory, though it was bang in front of our house. Trespassers would not be prosecuted for walking on it – whereas if they went through the Gathorne gate…!!! Moreover, the Fire Hydrant was always there, an unchanging part of the scenery. Whenever I peeped out into Mutton Lane, there it was. Whenever I jumped off the No. 29 bus and dashed across the road homeward, there it was again. To greet me. Not, strictly speaking, part of our domain but, unstrictly speaking, it was indeed part of home. A veritable marker of 301, an us-marker, standing fair and square outside our place.

So, it was a sheer delight for me when, very briefly, I caught sight of it again so many years into what was then the future. In 1991 I went, with one of my daughters and her children, to visit England including Potters Bar and, yes, 301 itself. To show my flesh and blood, 'This is my home, the best of all the homes I've ever had.' Though there have been a few others dear to me: Forestdale in Southgate, for instance, and one or two during my life abroad – in Benghazi, Khartoum and Alexandria – there's no question, 301 will always have pride of place. Not the least of my thrill, on seeing it again after decades, was to find the Fire Hydrant still there! Exactly the same, in exactly the same place, as it had always been. So much else had changed, practically everything else in fact; so many people had gone – so, so many. But the Fire Hydrant remained. Proving that all had not been lost. Providing a real and solid link – between those remote beloved days and this now and here. Bless it.

The Knitting Episode

Early on in the "infants", they decided to teach us to knit. The girls of course. In those day, the concept of gender discrimination hadn't yet been dreamed up. Though surely it must have occurred to some people: why shouldn't girls be trained in, say, woodwork? Or maybe some boys would like to have a bash at say embroidery – but if any boys did, they'd probably be instantly labelled 'gay' – though that was certainly non-discussable then and the adjective used was 'queer': that marvellous word 'gay' had not yet been so regrettably kidnapped.

So, for better or for worse, we girls were all presented with some wool and a pair of needles, whether we liked it or not.

And I did not. Moreover felt I had to make this quite clear. But how? Then I had a brilliant idea. 'Deeds rather than words.' Therefore, with the equipment provided, I produced something knitted – a travesty, no less, of what knitting was supposed to be. I'm wondering now, how on earth did I manage to "create" this travesty? To do so required a real grasp of the techniques of knitting – perhaps I had absorbed them, in my role of Chewdless, watching Mother's expert purling and plaining while I 'hairdressed'.

Whatever the explanation, the class teacher simply didn't know what to make of it, or of me, and sent me to Miss Dowling, the headmistress. Perhaps she'd have the know-how to deal with this quite unprecedented aberration from the norm.

I don't recall exactly what Miss Dowling said but at any rate there was no reprimand. Nothing more censorious than 'Why did you do this?' She might well have added, 'And how did you do it?' I bet none of the teachers gathered in the staff room could have produced anything like it – they might have benefited from a demonstration! Whatever, curiosity must have been uppermost in all their minds, 'Why had this funny little girl played this funny little trick?'

I could in theory have answered that question but in practice it was undoable. How could I have protested, 'Of course I can knit! It's not all that difficult – why, my mother does it practically without looking, while she reads books and magazines. But I don't want to spend my time, my energy, knitting. I'm not cut out for that. I prefer other much more interesting things.' Such as making up playgames and acting in them – my pastime of choice, and other kids, such as Marion, latched on to it. My sort of activities were so much more fun than theirs: pretending to do what housewives did. Who wanted to be a housewife anyway? That was the crux of it.

I certainly couldn't have told those teachers the deeper truth – that, even then, I rejected the feminine role, the woman's role – without, I reckon, even knowing that I rejected it. I just felt 'That's not me.' I never wanted to do what most of the other girls did – fool around with dolls, play 'mothers and fathers' or 'house' – I hated all that. It was so boring, so ordinary! It's a rejection I've maintained in one way or another all my life. Despite marriage, despite having children, grandchildren and, eventually great-grandchildren. Despite becoming a matriarch, in fact. But not a feminine matriarch! I suppose it doesn't add up, doesn't make sense. At any rate, I couldn't begin to explain all this to Miss Dowling, let alone to myself.

A year or so later, I got to know her a little. Her homeward path coincided with mine so some days she walked along with me as far as 301.

And we talked along too. I especially recall one conversation – about Finns and Russians. It was 1941 – our lanes and gardens all deeply blanketed in snow, reminding us of Finland and Russia who were having battles and skirmishes before the war proper on the eastern front got under way. Again, Miss Dowling might have thought *Who is this funny little girl? Following the news so keenly, just like an adult.* Echoing my classmates who used to tell me (in their case, in tones of reproach), 'You talk like a grown-up.' Well, what did they expect? Only child that I was (though later I acquired beloved siblings), surrounded by my elders, the apple of all their eyes. Not only joining in their talk as an equal (few concessions if any were needed to make it easy for me), their uncensored views being aired around me all the time. Lapping up their programmes too on the wireless.

So, I walked easily along with the headmistress; she was just another grown-up, after all. Most of the kids would shy away from any extra-mural one-to-one contact with teachers, head or other. Though even I was more than a little overawed by Mr Sims, the headmaster, the undoubted supremo – one memorable instance of this I've chronicled in the piece called 'Pivotal Point' (qv).

But – back to knitting. An amazing sequel to that childhood incident took place in the fullness of time. In later life, I actually came to enjoy this activity. I found the sheer process of plaining and purling very satisfying and soothing to the nerves. Certainly, a lot more so than smoking. It provided something to do with one's hands while watching TV, or listening to the radio, or even chatting with friends. And at the same time it was 'creative' or at any rate productive. Here was fabric I was manufacturing myself, almost without noticing, or exerting much effort. At first I would knit lots of squares, then I'd stitch them together and – lo and behold, a piece of material which I could fashion into a garment. I did this several times, designing and actually making some quite wearable clothes for myself and my children. As well as some coverings for chairs. Made me feel like Yves St Laurent! And by the way, doing such "womanly" work didn't turn him into a housewife, did it?

Which all goes to show – it's so vital the way a subject is introduced to a learner, even a child in primary school. Especially, a child in primary school. This can apply to anything – arithmetic, languages, or even sport. Any subject can be presented as a rewarding pursuit, with entertaining or intriguing aspects. Rather than as something difficult and/or unpleasant that you've got to do whether you like it or not. And, moreover, with no bearing on your life. Take trigonometry, for instance…No wonder kids balk at that. Unless they're little Einsteins in the making! Now, what if he'd been told in school, 'Get on with the woodwork!' Perhaps he was! Or what if they'd thrust on him needles and wool…! Well you never know, eventually – 'in the fullness of time' – even he might have got around to knitting himself some (much needed) socks. That doesn't necessarily preclude dreaming up $E = mc^2$. Does it?

The Persecution of Ig

Bullying was not unknown at Cranborne. I did my share of it. For some reason, for a very short period, I was elected leader of a gang – it certainly wasn't because of any physical prowess of mine. Let alone leadership qualities; those I signally lacked. Or eagerness to get into fights – on the contrary, I shrank from that – though now and then it was unavoidable. We called our gang a 'guild' – a rose by any other name. In fact we were just a group, about six or seven of us, with a few things in common; it had seemed natural to 'gang up together'. Though this automatically, if unintentionally, brought us into conflict with others.

We used to spend a lot of time in each other's company, both in school and out. We'd often stroll around the streets en masse. No particular aim in view – though we did invent some rather silly and pointless "projects". The main thing was just being together, ripe for any fun that might come our way. But it wasn't only fun that did that. Problems did too. Once we were wandering around a building site – we were particularly attracted to building sites; there was something fascinating about them, places where people were scheduled to live but were not yet doing so – a bit like Pompeii in reverse. There, we were faced with piles of paving stones about to be laid. This triggered a "project" – one of our silliest. The majority of 'guild' members decided that no such mundane or pedestrian measures as walking around these stones should be tolerated – instead, we must jump from the top of one pile to that of the next, and so on till they were all "done". Not surprisingly, timid as I was (and by no means an athlete) I demurred at that, but a guild member remarked reprovingly, 'I think the leader should be the first to do it.' Dread verdict! No arguing with it! So, heart in mouth, I bloody well did. Without mishap, praise be. But mission not yet accomplished – four more piles lay ahead, to be similarly "done". Mercifully, the guild collectively had second thoughts – no doubt perceiving that each of them would have to perform likewise – and a consensus was reached (we were nothing if not democratic). 'OK. Once is enough.' Rarely, have I been so relieved to be let off a hook. So much for being a leader!

Such physical ordeals weren't the only traps we fell into. Others were a good deal more unpleasant – harmful too. Worst of these was: we delighted in denigrating some of our classmates. Just about any non-guild-member was eligible. Some of them – people we liked, despite the ganging-up process – were exempted, and actually offered honorary membership; these included Rosemary (odd that she hadn't joined in the first place) and another favourite, Margaret Wood, and to their credit they declined.

Ridicule was our main weapon and we used it ruthlessly. Though we looked upon many as beyond the pale, some were distinctly more so than others. The furthest beyond of all was a girl whom I'll call 'Sally Igbert'. We downright tormented her. I in particular did so because of her name, reducing it to 'Ig'. This syllable I considered the epitome of ugliness. I gave her hell through it. It was I who started this persecution but the rest of the gang followed suit. Looking back now, aghast, I ask myself: didn't it occur to me that 'Ig' was the exact echo of the dominant sound in my own name, Briggs? – about which I'd long felt uncomfortable. I yearned to have a beautiful or even just an average-sounding name. Like Randall, say, or Stockbridge, or Morris, or Wood…You name it, everyone, yes everyone, in the class had a more euphonic name than mine and I would gladly have swapped with any of them, including Sally. 'Projection' was what it must have been, I learned from a shrink friend many years later – when also I realised I could easily soften and beautify 'Briggs' by adding my second name, Lesley, or my married one, Sharaf – either did the trick admirably.

However, that was far into the future and for that horrible now and there I persisted in tormenting Sally, aggressively hailing her as 'Ig!' Stressing the ugliness of the sound – all the guild members following my lead.

At that tender age – about seven or eight – supposed by some to be the age of reason – I felt no guilt whatsoever. But boy do I feel it now. Poor Sally – what had she done to deserve our bullying? Such a very nasty form of it too. Absolutely nothing – except not qualifying as 'one of us'. And why indeed should she have aspired to that? She was quite content to belong to no group, gang or guild or whatever, just to be herself. Albeit her lone self. Now, I recognise it was she who had something we lacked, and not vice versa. She didn't need to fill a void – but we did. We were the ones with inner emptiness to cope with.

No, not 'poor Sally'. Definitely not. She grinned and bore it, with nothing less than stoicism it seems to me with hindsight. She could have hit back, telling us, 'So what? I'm Big Ig – not like you miserable little whippersnappers.' But she uttered not a word of reproach. As if turning the other cheek. In hindsight, too, I take my hat off to her.

I'm more than happy that this most unpleasant phase in my school life didn't go on for very long. The whole thing couldn't have lasted more than a few months. The war was getting closer by the hour, giving us other, greatly more important things to concern ourselves with. And do. Worthwhile projects instead of silly pointless ones. And more worthwhile adversaries, more deserving enemies, on whom to vent any pent-up nastiness.

At least this miserable episode taught me something: if you must have someone to persecute, someone to hurt, go for one who deserves it. One moreover bigger than you, someone who can hit back and hurt back. Like, say, Hitler. Instead of the defenceless, go for the bully. And the bigger the better.

Otherwise, it's just too ignoble.

Mr Magnus

One's neighbours are like one's relatives – you don't choose them. Like them or lump them, you're stuck with them. Unlike friends. And this is something hard to check when considering a new home. Paying money, signing a contract, actually moving in – you might regret all that fortissimo if you find the next-door bastards unliveable with. There's an Arabic proverb I came across in Egypt:

El gar abla el dar = First the neighbour, then the house. So it was more than a stroke of luck that the sharers of our semi-detached happened to be, far from neighbours from hell, precisely the reverse.

They weren't just 'nice'. The head of their household, Marion's father, was a remarkable person on several counts. Once met, never forgotten. I call him 'Mr Magnus'. His real name had a truly Latin ring to it, Londoner though he was, East Ender at that. Well, there are other cases; some Brits are actually surnamed 'Caesar'. So a Latin pseudonym is quite appropriate for him, the most suitable I could think of being 'Mr Magnus'. For the best of reasons: he was great.

Question: What was so great about him? Answer: His talent.

Q: And what was that, exactly?

A: He had an extraordinary gift for composing word puzzles – anagrams, acrostics, complete crosswords even. Yet his job was – a driver on the London Underground.

He used to tell us how, as he was driving, clues and conundrums kept popping up in his mind – as he steered his train through the subterranean labyrinths of Russell Square, Covent Garden, Caledonian Road – then on and out into the open after Southgate, on to Enfield West (as Oakwood used to be called) and Cockfosters at the end of the Piccadilly Line. There the No. 29 bus would be waiting to take him home – where he belonged, next door to us, 303 to our 301. If his Tube passengers had known about that preoccupation of his, they might easily have been anxious. But – not to worry! He was so skilled at his day-job that his train could well be running on automatic pilot.

He hadn't had much of an education, and he knew what a drawback that was. He knew that, had he been placed differently in life, differently born, he might have had opportunities galore, gone far. How far, one wonders? Well, he might have become, say, a columnist on one of the papers, on one of his specialised subjects. He might even have risen up to equal Ximenes or Torquemada, grandmasters of the cryptic crossword. Or he might have pioneered something new. After all, Sudoku is but a recent innovation and, amazing as it seems now, crosswords themselves were not invented till the 1920s. Much as we may have pictured people doing them while relaxing in the Titanic's deck chairs.

Lack of education and culture had imposed limits on what he could do with his talent; it was thwarted; he'd missed out, embedded as he was in the working class, from the East End, moreover. In fact it was through him and his family that I first learned what 'East End' meant – the poorest part of the City, the hinterland of St. Paul's, that bore the brunt of the Blitz and what the Queen Mother referred to (then she was simply The Queen) when she said, 'Now we can look the East End in the eye' – this after some shrapnel had hit the walls of Buckingham Palace. She didn't have to apologise: she and her husband assiduously visited every single one of the blitzed areas. Emphasising how we were all in it together – 'From the Ritz/to the Anchor and Crown', as Noël Coward has so memorably put it. Class wasn't relevant. Upper, middle, royal, common – you name it. All in it together.

Mr Magnus wasn't bitter. He'd realised early on that to make it with that talent of his you need truckloads of culture. And that meant books. So he filled his home with them. However, he didn't get them the way we did – walk into W.H. Smiths and buy some – but via some cut-price offers in the papers, Co-op-wise. He applied for those and got them, lots of them – encyclopaedias and atlases as well as mere tomes. How I longed to be let loose in his front room and burrow through them all! We too saw such adverts, but never did anything about them – anyway, Granddad had all the books he needed. Longfellow, Tennyson, Dickens, et al, et al, et al, the family bookcase was full to the brim with them, had been since his early married days. I burrowed through those all right and, in addition, he read to me selectively from them; not just the famous stuff but the more obscure. A book called *Sable and White* – name of author forgotten – was our mutual favourite; it purported to be the autobiography of a dog, the sort of story that rarely failed to attract Brit readership, hooked on dogs as most folk in England were. And still are, it seems.

For the Magnuses, the Co-op was the key. Determining their lifestyle. They got most of their purchases that way, including groceries. Every Saturday they would board the 29 for a trip to Turnpike Lane, site of a big store (forerunner of supermarkets) and stock up with their week's supplies. No frequenter of Turnpike myself, it lies beyond the Gathorne/Wood Green stamping ground, though my parents, during their courtship days, were ardent Tottenham Hotspur fans, and often passed through there on their way to the stadium at White Hart Lane. Up the Spurs!

We too belonged to the Co-op – we got our wartime rations there, we had our number and drew our 'dividend' – again, my first encounter with a word. But we didn't take it as seriously as the Magnuses did; we were moderate about it, maybe because we were Conservatives (and not with a small c at that) whereas they were out-and-out Labour. Whatever – in the East End you learn the hard way, you have to be penny-wise. Or else.

Little did I imagine, when strolling home with Rosemary from our elocution class of a Saturday morning, we passed the Co-op store, that she would devote the greater part of her life to that organisation. Seeing in it what she at one time sought in politics, and didn't find – a way of building the new 'Jerusalem / in England's green and pleasant land'. Casting aside for it those other 'callings' of hers, in which she'd excelled so brilliantly – her molecular biology, and her poetry. Little indeed could Rosemary herself have foreseen such a sacrifice – far, far into the future as it then lay.

I was intrigued by the Magnus's way of life and how it differed from ours. I used to think, *Theirs is so much more fun!* I would often pop into their place, to be with Marion; in their kitchen, her ma would ply me with some goodies they'd got from Turnpike. Tasty stuff! But fun and cornflakes weren't the only aspects of good neighbourliness.

Suburban values dictate that you rarely, if ever, penetrate your neighbour's home; in this context they do apply to Potters Bar as well as to most of Greater London. But not the East End. There, everyone mucks in together.

Ah, but come the war, and all that changed!

There was a wooden fence between our two backyards. Hostilities had barely started when Mr Magnus cut a gap in it, so we could run through and share their Anderson air-raid shelter, installed in the garden below ground level to protect against blast. (There were Morrison shelters too, for use indoors, stout metal tables you slept under. Both were named after government ministers). That gap in the fence was a thrilling symbol for me – making it seem we really were one family. How I wished we were!

I couldn't have felt more 'kith and kin' with Marion had she been my twin sister; we were born to be close. We needed each other. Me an only child surrounded by adults – albeit adoring ones; she the only girl among brothers. We were about the same age – she four, me five, when we first met.

When she called me from her garden with her special call, 'Iroo!' I'd rush out instantly to our shared fun. We had such a lot of it. We would immerse ourselves in our 'playgames' – nothing should interrupt them, not even Mr Chamberlain declaring war! I made them up and "directed" them, and we co-starred; our hero and heroine, á la William Powell and Myrna Loy, were called Dan and Gloria – for some reason these were the sexiest names I could think of. These little mini-dramas were as compelling as any soap, based on far-from-real-life situations. (What did we know about 'real life'?). A certain Mini Mauri was the baddy – we did her lines too, taking turns, since there was no third player to hand.

No 'mothers and fathers' crap for us! Much less 'he', or 'hopscotch' – chasing about, exhausting ourselves, and for what? Damn all.

All this gave Marion a sort of pleasure she could only find with me. You might even call it happiness.

It wasn't all one-way traffic, though. She taught me things, useful things like how to ride a bike. After hours of her patient steering, what a thrill when I found myself suddenly going alone! A skill that's served me well throughout life; I made good use of it well into middle age.

Mr Magnus and Granddad were similarly close. Despite the class difference, the Labour/Tory divide – that didn't seem to matter one iota compared with what they had in common. Not the least of this was a shared interest in gardening. Though Granddad was a very hard act to follow, Mr Magnus did his best. (Some plants, like syringa, grew on both sides of the railings that separated the gardens and received mutual care). And their almost daily get-togethers included his regularly popping in to cut Granddad's hair.

Once, they had a row! Granddad had complained about the noise from their wireless. 'It's like a fairground!' Another area where Eastenders are unlike suburbanites – noise doesn't bother them; on the contrary, they seem to thrive on it. That was the only time I'm aware of where a difference caused a clash. For a very short while they weren't on speaking terms and Marion whispered to me she'd been told 'not to play with Iris'. But it only lasted two days!

Yes, those things that might have divided them, made them the coolest of neighbours, were very much outweighed by what they had in common. And those were big things. One of them was having missed out. Granddad too could have gone so much further than he had – with that university potential of his that had perforce remained unrealised. But he too wasn't bitter. He let such feelings be sublimated into his love of books and his real ability to pass on as much knowledge as he possibly could – especially to me.

But even more of a bond between these two men, these two fathers, was their shared experience of tragedy. On Granddad's side was the terrible pain when my mother was pronounced incurably ill, mentally, and incarcerated in hospital – with, at first, no prospect of release. And even after her eventual (against the odds) discharge, doubt and concern remained about her future, her marriage having broken up forever.

This catastrophe was paralleled on Mr Magnus's side by the loss of his eldest son, drowned in the reservoir at Ponders End. He never spoke about this; neither did his wife. Did Shakespeare ever speak – or write – about his lost son Hamnet? Some griefs go too deep for words, no matter what language one may have at one's command.

The Magnuses were a pair ideally suited. It showed. I could not but admire their wedding photo in pride of place on their mantelpiece. What a handsome pair! Their Christian names happened to be Will and Kate – how Shakespearean can you get? And indeed Will did resemble Laurence Olivier who was starring nationwide then as Henry-V, while Kate was beautiful with the high-cheekboned look of a top Stratford actress playing the Shrew. She was tender-hearted to a fault; she wept copiously when our beloved grandmother died. Observing our family at such close range, she understood how very much more than a mother surrogate my darling grandma had been to me. And, these days, I've come to believe that caring for me then, already in her sixties, with all the responsibility entailed and all the anxiety – mark you, that was much worse then than it is now after the advent of so much immunisation non-existent then. Not to mention the actual work. All this may well have induced the stroke she suffered and thereby shortened her life.

Like many of my friends' parents, Will and Kate felt sorry for me. They didn't say so to my face, but I felt it. And it hurt – made me think, *They must have good reason.* They probably dubbed me 'broken-home kid', my parents' marriage having unravelled irreparably when Mum was pronounced incurable and hospitalised for such a long time. Oddly enough, she and Dad remained 'amicable' – but he, understandably, had found someone else. Who dug her claws in and wouldn't let go. For a while, it seems to me, Mum didn't know about this; for a while, she was hoping he was looking around for a new home for the three of us. But – time passed and that didn't happen; at some point – maybe someone told her, maybe she just intuited and realised what a hopeless scenario she'd been envisaging. And gave up: and moved on to the next phase – finding someone else herself.

I didn't feel this as a hardship or handicap in those blessed Cranborne days. Especially as Daddy never, never failed to visit me, giving up every one of his hard-earned Saturdays to be with me. Whether his new "consort" liked it or not. She knew damn well she'd have to put up with it – that was the price tag affixed to her 'relationship'; there was no question of not paying it. And pay up she did – and kept him.

I only recognised the situation as the disaster it was several years later. In the Cranborne days, with such marvellous more-than-parents as Granny and Granddad, and my wonderful aunts, Mother's sisters – I was the apple of all their eyes. Sid's too – my wondrous Uncle (comrade of Pat Garland, Jack Hawkins, et al). I certainly didn't feel "deprived" – I felt exactly the opposite. I thought, *what does it matter if Mum and Dad have split up?* But Will and Kate and the others, Rosemary's parents among them, saw that it did matter – a very great deal.

***

Marion and I, Will and Granddad, those weren't the only pairs of cross-garden chums. Like most suburbanites, we had pets, and 'Pal Magnus' was the staunch buddy of 'Bob Rodwell'. His barked equivalent of 'Iroo!' had our own dear pooch bounding out immediately to join him in canine 'playgames'.

Bob was truly a member of the Rodwell clan, not only faithful guardian especially of me, since the days I was in my pram. He was indeed one of us 'in sickness and in health', in peace and war, in joy and pain. One dark winter night a cat scratched out one of his eyes. And he always pined if my mother was away from home even for a few days – like all the animals in her life (and there were many) he loved her deeply and she him. He was finally laid to earth there in the 301 garden, by Granddad's shed. By his very presence staking a claim on our behalf. Custodian of our right – like any member of any diaspora, Arab or Jew or whatever, to return to, or at least revisit, the long-lost Holy Land.

The Fair

We didn't often have fairs in Potters Bar. Fêtes, now, were another matter, quite run-of-the-mill; often some society or other would put one on in aid of this or that charity. Not much fun, nothing out of the ordinary – buying raffle tickets or home-made goodies, targeting Aunt Sallies. Apart from the odd fortune-teller, nothing very intriguing. But fairs – they were in a category apart. Higher profile, much bigger deal. Hardware as opposed to soft. For one thing, there was machinery involved. Dangerous machinery sometimes – people could get killed. That happened once at the top of Mutton Lane where a fair had been set up, with sundry fun-geared apparatus installed. In a big field facing the billboard and ads corner. This was the place to advertise your product (equivalent of prime time, i.e. prime site). I passed it every time I went to and from Sunday school – one poster in particular I recall, about an anti-vivisection society and I diligently memorised its address in Victoria Street – and another saying 'A vote for him (the local Tory candidate) is a vote for him' – meaning Churchill. (Despite these countrywide exhortations, not to mention winning the war, he lost that post-war election).

But I digress! 'All the fun of the fair' was being promised – outdoing Widdecombe and Scarborough Fairs combined. The public eagerly watched as a high-tech merry-go-round, mother of all murderous whirligigs, was put in place. Strapped into those violently revolving chairs, swirling around and around, high up, you wouldn't stand much of a chance if something went wrong. Which it did. One of the chairs worked loose and, with its human cargo, hurtled some furlongs to crash-land in a neighbouring meadow. A minor tragedy, it hardly made it into the town's annals, compared say with the railway disaster of May 2002 or the shot-down Zeppelin of 1918, but it remained unforgettable for those who'd been close to it. Enough to make one boycott such whirligigs forever.

Even so, fairs still drew us like magnets. Promise of magic. Such an occasion marked what I have to call one of the most remarkable days of my life. One of the happiest, even.

It took place in the old part of town, where the Cuffley Road – venue of posh and celeb residents – zooms in to join the A1000-cum-Great North Road-cum-Potters Bar High Street. Here is the nucleus of the town; from this place it started out as a small village, a long time ago. A very long time ago. Pre-1066, pre-Domesday Book, maybe even before Wyllyott's Manor was built (listed as it is in Domesday). Pride of our neck of the woods, just off Darkes Lane (was that in existence then, along with ditto Mutton?) And just who was Darke? Or Darkes, was it? A prominent personality, no doubt. And as for Wyllyott – he must have been a Saxon big shot. No, Wyllyotts wasn't the nucleus in those far-off days, just the moderately stately home of pre-Norman nabobs, a 'manor' suitably insulated from the hoi polloi. Only a stone's throw from it, open fields prevailed then and continued to prevail till our arrival on the scene in 1933.

In fact, it was around that time, the '30s, that the town's nucleus did begin to gravitate towards the Wyllyotts area. After nigh on a thousand years the quasi stately home came into its own – purpose-built, it appeared at last, as a municipal headquarters. Just the right place to install a telephone exchange or have gas masks tested – which Granny and I did there after the Munich crisis in 1938, despite those hopes of 'peace in our time'. And in more recent years it has come even further into its own as a community centre. Wyllyotts was more or less on our doorstep, while that other, original nucleus was more than a good mile off. But we would gladly have tramped leagues to get to The Fair.

So it was that one marvellous summer's day I found myself there, with Rosemary, and, of course, her mother, who chaperoned her everywhere. I don't say this in any spirit of censure – far from it. If she seemed over-protective I can well understand – I believe Rosemary had been fragile in early infancy and probably she still was. I guess that was why she didn't start school till aged six, while I and most others did so at five. Thus she began her academic life a year after me – but continued it many years longer, acquiring accolade upon accolade, whereas I dropped out aged fifteen. Yes, her Ma had reason enough to be protective and not only that. Potters Bar was not without its fair share of hazards; there were murderers on the loose, including one serial killer, and so were child molesters – as proven when Marion and I were confronted with one when strolling near Bridgefoot. (See piece entitled "How not to earn five bob").

But I digress again! 'All the fun of the fair!' What an understatement! While I was pottering about with Rosemary, *y su mama tambien*, who should we bump into but, of all people, Derek Stockbridge. None other than he, the handsomest of our classmates, the great love of my Cranborne life, eclipsing all other – the "real thing", graduated to after the Mr Bath 'apprenticeship'. The perfectly innocent "real thing", I must stress. There was nothing, but nothing, about sex in it. Especially delightful too – Derek was accompanied by his best friend, John Morris. A person I both liked and admired – for a very good reason. The kids had more than once taunted him:

"You love Iris Briggs".

Far from denying this, he'd stood his ground, quite unruffled, and answered them levelly,

'Yes, I do.'

I was impressed by that. It took courage. Being in love was something you could be persecuted for in school those days. It exposed you to ridicule. Why, I wonder? Perhaps because it proves you have sexual feelings – something to be hushed up at all costs. Or because it renders you vulnerable, prone to making a fool of yourself...?

I don't know.

Another would-be swain of mine was Ronald Cox. Of all the graffiti abounding in our neighbourhood, for me the most striking was:

'Ronald Cox loves Iris Briggs.'

Emblazoned on a fence near Darkes Lane, for all the world to see – or at least all Potters Bar! No need for 'media'!

I felt appreciative and, yes grateful to Ronald, as well as John. Both those males – albeit ten-year-olds at the time – did my ego a power of good. And not just then – in the future as well. Providing much-needed proof that there was indeed in me something that the opposite sex felt drawn to – despite my own strong feelings and urges to the contrary (witness 'The Knitting Episode'). That I wasn't just 'Timmy' as I'd been dubbed in babyhood, probably because of some male traits in me obvious even then, far less the 'idiot boy' some saw in me even as an adult. These included a 'shrink' who knew me well, and to cap it all, my very husband. ('Yes, I see what he means,' the shrink had said!) Moreover, I myself can see it, plain as a pikestaff – the unfeminine, it's definitely there. Not playing with dolls, no truck with 'mother and father' games, I never really saw myself as a woman **and** I still don't. Although in due course I became a wife and mother, then grandmother and even great-grandmother…But a woman? A mind, a person that's me. Nevertheless, I never wanted to be written off as unattractive per se. Hence the unashamedly declared love of those two boys was a precious shot in the arm – and still is. It can still boost my self-confidence in times of insecurity. So I'm forever grateful to Ronald and John.

I hardly knew Ronald; he was in a different cohort from mine – one up or down, I forget. John, however, I knew well. He was the scion of Bridge House – top eatery and hostelry, bestriding Mutton Lane as it overlooks the railway. He was one of the very few who used to cycle to and from school. One of the élite; well-off, with the appropriate trappings, of which a bike was the most modest. Ideal best friend for Derek, perfectly offsetting my Rosemary. In fact, wouldn't the two of them have been just right as best man and bridesmaid in the unlikely event of…? So unlikely I didn't even fantasise about it. Then. But now I do, occasionally.

I don't recall anything of what we did at The Fair. Or even any of our conversation there. Except at one point, Derek remarked to me, 'Are you stony broke?' Implying a certain intimacy. A certain caring! How I savoured that!

He must have guessed I was hard up, as I was hesitating to splurge on some desired object. Did he lend me five bob or so? A fiver would have been way beyond our pocket money income bracket. And we certainly didn't go on any of the whirligigs. Sufficient fun it was for me just being with Derek, backed up – like an ideal supporting cast – by our truly best friends, John and Rosemary. Just being together, the four of us, was what it was all about.

Did the others relish it as I did? Did John, in love with me as he was, savour to the utmost just being in my presence, get the same kick as I did out of that chance magic meeting? Did any of them, like me play it over and over in their memory during the subsequent years and decades? Can they still do that? Are they still around? Rosemary passed on in 2003, when the war in Iraq was about to begin; her cremation took place on St Valentine's Day that year, the day preceding the famous Saturday of anti-war protests. Anti-war – a theme dearest to her heart.

At long last it was time to go home. And on that mile-long trek I had an attack of something that never before or since troubled me in my Cranborne days – a very urgent need to urinate. Barely able to trudge along with Rosemary and her mum, by the time we reached the 'pivotal point' – (see piece of this name) I thought I'd had it and would have to lose face in front of them by wetting my pants. Fortunately, it was only a few yards to 301 and the blessed relief of the loo. But even if that unwelcome scenario had come about, it would have been a price worth paying for such a superlative day. The Day of the Fair – I repeat, one of the best of my life and, yes, truly one of the happiest.

New Tel Aviv

There's a lot of difference between Potters Bar and Southgate, where I moved for four years to attend the grammar school, Southgate County, following my father's tradition. He was a pupil there in WWI. The two municipalities are separated by the Green Belt surrounding London; when that was established the word 'green' had not yet acquired its current meaning, but the implication was the same. The most striking feature of the Belt was and still is Stagg Hill – surely the steepest hill I've ever seen in my life. As a result of this 'green' barrier, Southgate forms part of Greater London, well and truly a suburb of the capital, whereas Potters Bar is not (a difference further stressed later when that other divider, the M25, came into being) and has to be classified as 'Home Counties'.

There are other differences, and some of them hit you in the eye. For instance, Southgate is 'cosmopolitan'; it's obviously part of a major capital city, rather than typifying 'little England' to which Potters Bar can fairly be said to belong. In Southgate foreigners abound. So do Jews, whereas in Potters Bar they were few and far between – I can only think of two in the whole town – Melsen, a newly installed confectioner and Izod the estate agent. In some parts of Southgate you could be forgiven for assuming Jews outnumbered gentiles – Forestdale, where we settled, was among the streets with the highest quota. In fact this leafiest of leafy suburbs could have run Golders Green a close second for the title 'New Tel Aviv'.

I found this quite delightful and stimulating. Something refreshingly novel and I took to it like the proverbial duck to water. At school, for a good while my closest friend was Jewish Ruth. Furthermore, I developed a crush on her handsome brother, Jules. He was, I think, barely aware of my existence, grubby little ink-stained blue stocking that I was then; my feelings were even more unrequited than most schoolgirl crushes are – like, for instance, my previous one on Mr Bath. However, I was a frequent visitor at Ruth's home (and incidentally the best Christmas party I ever attended was hosted there by her parents). It was quite a long way from Forestdale and I remember her mother giving me the bus fare to get home quickly – to save time and energy for the looming hours of homework. I bore this in mind whenever anyone voiced that widely-held prejudice, 'Jews are mean' – as absurd and groundless as the similar one about Scots.

Ruth's home was outstanding too for another 'best ever' – namely a collection of gramophone records duly catalogued card-index-wise (no computers then). I was utterly entranced by it, especially the opera component. Gigli, Caruso, Patti, Tetrazzini – all the giants of the early twentieth century, the pioneering stars of the recording era. My discovery of all this at Ruth's took place, mind you, at the height of the war when Italian, and German, music was viewed by some "patriots" as enemy alien culture. This attitude caused me much distress, as I had already fallen in love with Italian opera – along with Italy itself, Rome and everything Roman and Latin; indeed the very fact of being at war with Italy was a real source of pain for me. I agonised about all the archaeological and artistic treasures being exposed to bombardment, not to mention the singers and other musicians. True, efforts were made to spare 'cultural monuments' and that term covered some of the leading performers, among them Toscanini and Gigli. For these reasons alone (even if for no other, which of course was not the case) I longed for the war to be over. In the meantime, Ruth's gramophone collection kept me going opera-wise, nurturing what was to become a life-long passion.

Southgate had several other Jewish citizens who made a strong impression on me. For instance, the people next-door to us in Forestdale. Our gardens were linked, as with the Magnuses and the famous gap in the fence, by the theme of air-raid shelters. Here there were two. Theirs and ours; each was half in one territory and half in the other. Ours was covered throughout the summer by a canopy of cornflowers – a touch of sweet beauty ironically stemming from the hideousness of war. Our neighbours were very cordial. They held a wedding in their garden and invited us. The bride was from Vienna while the groom, they told us, was 'a Palestinian Jew'. Even then, quite a few years before the founding of Israel and all the subsequent turmoil in the Middle East, and even more years before my own "emigration" to that part of the world and consequent hyperawareness of all the news about it, that term, 'a Palestinian Jew', struck me as being an oxymoron.

Other Hebraic neighbours abounded. My favourite was Mrs Lipton, an elderly lady who sometimes popped in for a chat with Ma, and on the births of my siblings brought home-made goodies as gifts – a custom I came across later in the Middle East among Arabs and Jews alike. Mrs Lipton made light of any anti-Semitism she may have come up against (and believe me, there was no lack of it) joking with us about the Black Market – how if Jewish perpetrators were involved it got much more coverage. Her daughter, another Ruth, was indeed an impressive figure, no gentile more glamorous than she in her WVS* uniform, itself a very becoming outfit worthy of some top designer. Doing their bit for England which they all saw not as their adoptive country but their real one. Each felt her/himself to be one of us and was accepted as such. Every inch as much a Londoner as, say, Stevie Smith the poet or Flora Robson the actress, also Southgate residents living near us.

Some days I would stroll with friends across a strip of blitzed wasteland where posters advertised a show starring *Issy Bon, the Hebrew Comedian.* Triggering our cheeky response, 'Is he bon? No, he's lousy.'

In our district the number of synagogues to the square mile was way above the national average; though recently I've learned, from the ABC Atlas of London Streets, that other areas boast even higher quotas – for example Spitalfields, (Map 4 with its record number of synagogues to the square inch).

By contrast Potters Bar had no such facilities and little or no congregation to use them. Perhaps that's all changed now. Perhaps now it's full not only of Jews but also of Bangladeshis, Caribbeans, Nigerians, Ugandans – you name it. Perhaps mosques are springing up too, along with other 'temples'. Then, my native town was well and truly a bastion of WASPs – how Little England can you get? Now, I wonder, it's a bastion of – what? Multiculturalism? I doubt it!

All this goes to show what a difference a few miles and a very steep hill can make. Reminiscent of how, in New York, nothing separates Little Italy from China Town; they're cheek by jowl – in a moment you can kid yourself you're not in the same country, or the same continent even.

However, regrettably, lack of Jews didn't mean lack of anti-Semitism. Throughout my childhood in the '30s I overheard remarks reflecting this. Before and during the war epithets such as 'Jewboy' and 'shonk' were bandied about, even by "nice" people, such as some of our friends. As for the post-war times, I was shocked, ca. 1947, to find Oswald Mosely's* supporters holding forth in the

---

* WVS = Women's Voluntary Services
* Oswald Mosely. Erstwhile leader of British fascist party.

street behind Gloucester Road Underground station – a sort of poor man's Speaker's Corner – with racist ravings and sneering remarks about "the chosen people'. I was really amazed. 'What's this?' I asked myself. 'Haven't we won the war? Wasn't Hitler defeated?' Apparently, not entirely. His ideas, his ideology, seemed to have survived. And I fear they go on surviving, in some form or other, even to the present day.

Juanita and the Waxworks

Just a few houses down the road from my uncle's place in Southgate were neighbours who had taken in refugees from the Spanish Civil War. One of these was a girl called Juanita which, of course, Anglophone to a fault, we insisted on pronouncing 'Jewanita'. By contrast, she spoke remarkably good English. I wondered where she'd learned it – must have gone to a very good school in Spain? Afterwards it occurred to me that perhaps the Southgate people sheltering her – whom we didn't know very well – were relatives; maybe she'd lived a lot with them either here or in Spain and thereby become almost bilingual.

Though she was a few years older than me, we got on fine together. Noticing this was one of my mother's glamorous group of friends – arguably the most glamorous of the lot. Nurse Ball. She was exceptional for several reasons. Not least her partnership – which quickly transformed into marriage with one Gifford, a charismatic character in his own right. They were a pair to remember, by any standards. They had first met on the Underground – a launching pad, I guess, for quite a few lifetime liaisons. He'd lived many years in the Far East and acquired much of its culture, including expertise in such arts as origami. In this vein he produced a memorable entry for my autograph album, a design wrought by folding paper over blobs of oil paint, then rubbing the paper so as to make a distinctive pattern on the page.

Nurse Ball – I never found out her first name – it might have been Lucille for all I know! – was outstanding too for being very thoughtful and generous. Her birthday gift to me, contrasting with that of the Rev Argyll was *The Black Tulip*, by Alexandre Dumas. Its cover alone gave me much delight, and the very notion of a flower being black was fascinating. It was perceptive of Nurse Ball to realise that, primary school kid though I was, I'd highly appreciate such nuances.

Another of her kindnesses was to invite Juanita and me on a splendid London outing. Not just a single trip but a dual one. The first part comprised the Disney film *Snow White and the Seven Dwarfs*, then wowing the West End. The second was a visit to Madame Tussaud's.

Enriching as both these entertainments undoubtedly were, they are completely overshadowed in my memory by Juanita's comment,

'Where do they get the wax from? Out of people's ears?'

Fujihito Matsumori

At the height of WWII, it might have struck a neutral observer as odd that one of the most respected residents of Forestdale, leafiest lane in that leafiest of suburbs, Southgate, was Japanese – I'll call him Fujihito Matsumori. Way back, on a visit to UK, he'd married an Englishwoman and settled in London. He'd stayed on there, with their daughter – I'll call her Maureen – after her mother had died, sharing the home with his English sister-in-law. He'd secured for himself a good job in the City – and, I presume, become naturalised. He'd stayed on after the outbreak of WWII and even after Pearl Harbour.

He sent his daughter to my school. She was some classes my senior yet, despite the apartheid common between cohorts, we occasionally walked home together. She talked to me about Japan. I was enthralled. And I wondered, wasn't she homesick for it? It must have seemed extremely cut off then. What about her relatives there – and friends? Surely she missed them?

She was recognised as a brilliant pupil; this was very obvious when she took part in the debates of the Society for the Discussion of International Affairs. I recall one of her talks in which she used the 'beam and mote' allusion – I was impressed by her knowledge of things like that and wondered – was she equally familiar with such expressions in Japanese literature? At any rate she fitted very harmoniously into the school – hardly the enemy alien.

As for her father, he too was entirely 'integrated' (to use a word much in vogue nowadays). Complete with rolled umbrella and bowler hat, Daily Telegraph tucked under his arm, every day he would walk up and down Forestdale on his way to and from the City. Like all other commuters, taking bus and Underground. Few if any used cars then – they had them but, petrol being strictly rationed, most cars were stuck in their garages – every Forestdale house had one of these which was not the case in Mutton Lane – just one of the indices distinguishing upmarket from downmarket. Yes, Mr Matsumori was the epitome and stereotype of the successful London businessman.

Our neutral observer might have thought that, in the years sandwiched between Pearl Harbour and Hiroshima, places like Forestdale would be absolute no-go areas for such as he. Not a bit of it! He had thoroughly proved his Britishness – earned it the hard way, worked his passage home. Even the most jingoistic inhabitants of the leafy lane accepted him as 'one of us'. To the extent that he was enrolled on the ARP*roster of fire watchers, taking his turn to stay up all night, on the look-out. Doing his bit, just like the rest of us.

By stark contrast, a few houses further along, in a house commandeered by the government, a family of Belgian refugees had been billeted. Was not Belgium well and truly on our side? 'Shoulder to shoulder' with us in two world wars, backing us up against Hitler and the Kaiser alike. And what about Tintin and Simenon and above all Hercule Poirot? Shouldn't those 'gallant allies' of ours be welcomed into our midst with the utmost empathy, not to mention compassion?

Again, not a bit of it. On the contrary, these people were shunned, looked at askance, or simply ignored. 'Why? Whatever was the reason?' The neutral one would understandably ask. The answer, 'They just didn't fit in.' In Forestdale they were as alien as, say, Inuit or Sahara desert dwellers would have been. This showed in a myriad ways. First and foremost, the way they dressed: it marked them out as peasants. In England we don't have peasants – or haven't had for the past several centuries – town and country alike. The most rural of the rural are indistinguishable, dress wise, from the most urban of the urban. Peasants – definitely not the thing in the quintessential London that Forestdale epitomised. A far cry indeed from Mr Matsumori and his carefully acquired, fully integrated persona. In a nutshell – he conformed; they didn't.

It must be said, we knew very little about them. As individuals, nothing. And didn't want to know. Rumours, however, abounded. Some Forestdalers contended that they used the garden as a toilet: I can't corroborate this; I was a bit too far down the road to be able to ascertain, from an upstairs window, with or without binoculars, whether or not this was the case.

But, assuming it was – what was the big deal? Perhaps they thought they were doing us a favour – a way of saying 'thank you'. Repaying our hospitality – if such you can call it – by the only means available to them – fertilising their hosts' garden with the fruit of their labours, so to speak. What better fertiliser

---

* ARP = Air Raid Precautions

indeed? Peasants that they were, they well knew that human 'night soil' is even more nourishing for plants than mere manure. After all, they could observe practically every day how Fujihito's next-door-but-one (an ardent gardener) would rush out, trowel in hand, to scoop up the largesse every time a passing horse left his card.

However that might be, these Belgians were indubitably *personae non gratae*. Whatever they did or did not do. Asylum seekers take note. When it comes to 'integration' bear in mind: prejudice, racism, they're always there, albeit beneath the surface, and it doesn't take much to stir them up. At least in London – I can't vouch for other cities, only suspect. What I do know is: above all, you must look like us. You must not, on any account, stick out like a sore thumb.

Fujihito had realised that and accordingly done his homework. With such formidable cards stacked against him, he'd made the colossal, almost superhuman effort to trump them all. Even – most daunting of the lot – the 'slitty-eyed' look (to quote Prince Philip's not so bon mot.) One possible course might have been to pass as Chinese – in view of the adulation lavished then on the Chiang kai Sheks. But he'd scorned that option.

So many decades later, I wonder: when – if – he ever went back to Tokyo, how was he received there? I recalled Marlene Dietrich, so beloved of us throughout WWII, German equivalent of Maurice Chevalier, darling of Noël Coward, Lili Marlene personified – she wasn't exactly welcomed as a heroine in post-war Berlin.

Was it like that for Matsumori? Was he viewed as far from a hero in post-Hiroshima Japan? Could he indeed go back safely to his native land? Or was he fêted there as a champion – for a truly sensational tour de force, a spectacular mission accomplished, pulling the wool over our 'enemy' eyes so successfully, for such a very long time?

I fear we shall never know. But I can't help wondering. I really can't.

Rationing

In these days of TV kitchen gurus such as Delia Smith and Nigella Lawson, and with limitless ingredients from all over the world available in supermarkets, it's easy to bring recipes from the pages of a gourmet book to vivid life on the table. That wasn't the case in WWII. There was no such thing as supermarkets anyway and stuff from all over the world definitely was not available, thanks to German submarines, a.k.a. U-boats. They aimed to sink any ship they could spot that was bringing food to Britain.

But this menace had been foreseen and, like other measures to confront life-threatening dangers – notably air-raid shelters and gasmasks – all was arranged for every citizen well in advance of actual war. All the vital strategies had been thought through, and implemented, even pre-Munich. Not the least of these was rationing. It ensured that a fair share of essentials reached everyone, regardless of financial status. True, a few well-off individuals tried to get around the rules and siphon off extra supplies; such malpractice was known as the Black Market. It was seen as the most heinous of offences and dealt with accordingly.

Yes, everything had been thought of pre-Munich. So we weren't, in any area of our lives, forced to go short. Vital measures included the whole system of ration books and coupons, covering every commodity, every item of our diet (and it extended to clothing too). Even chocolate had been taken into account; you might think that was unimportant, a luxury people could do without. No so – even though we kids revelled in it as a treat, it had a more serious aspect, being part of the 'iron rations' we had to lug every day to school (along with our books and of course gas masks) in case we were stuck for hours in the shelters.

There was a memorable ad in the papers concerning this. Specifically, Fry's Chocolate Sandwich, a bar made up of alternating layers of plain and milk chocolate. Various celebs in squashed situations would remark, 'Speaking of sandwiches, have you tried Fry's Chocolate Sandwich?' I drew on this for an entry in a poster competition: Hitler, hopelessly wedged between the Red Army and the Western allies, both advancing on Berlin, pathetically enquires, 'And speaking of sandwiches, have you tried Fry's Chocolate Sandwich?'

Yes, everything had been thought of and done, pre-Munich. Hats off to the government of those times, i.e. that of Neville Chamberlain. For ensuring for everyone not only air-raid shelters and gasmasks but the very food we ate. No one went hungry, or even malnourished. Far from it; because everything was so well planned and carried out, people got just what they needed. Plus beneficial extras – things like rose hip syrup; few would have bothered with this or even heard of it before the war or if left to their own devices. But since there was allowance for it among our coupons we duly went to our local Food Office, conveniently located by the Catchpole Nurseries where Granddad regularly bought his plants and seeds – to get our share: since we were entitled to it, pity to forego it. So there were no pangs of hunger – and no obesity either. In fact, health levels throughout Britain were at an all-time high. Yes, hats off to that government.

I sometimes permit myself the heresy of thinking the real hero of the war was not Churchill but Chamberlain. 'Peace in our time.' If he'd been allowed to follow through on that pledge, so many people – many thousands, nay, millions – would have survived who did not. In Potters Bar alone, Ada and Ida, those maiden ladies, the Burgoyne grandchildren, the five Walsh children and their mother. And countrywide, people like Pat Garland and his RAF brothers. But…But…the Holocaust would have gone on unchecked, almost certainly crossing the Channel along with the Wehrmacht. And any one of us with a drop of Jewish blood would have been rounded up and trundled off to our own national Auschwitz. So – millions would not have survived, who did.

Sometimes, and very sadly, it seems you can't pin your faith on 'jaw-jaw' and it has to be 'war-war'. At any rate, few governments in the history of the world can have done more than Chamberlain's to protect and sponsor the health and safety of their people. And not the least part of that achievement was rationing.

***

Going to school those days wasn't an unmitigated pleasure. It wasn't very comforting when I came to that point in Forestdale where, before the road bends, I could look back and catch a last glimpse of No. 28, our home. I had to do this;

it was a compulsion, spurred by the thought, "*Who knows when, or if, we shall see each other again?* Probably kids going to school in Germany, and Russia, and Japan, were doing the self-same thing. Obsessive compulsive disorder (OCD) as shrinks call it, in the making; such 'neuroses' can last a lifetime. Another instance of this was – I had to place my gasmask in a certain position before getting into bed, otherwise I wouldn't be able to sleep.

Air raids can happen any time. They were more common – indeed, expected, by night. But in daytime too – you never knew. The V2s especially the Peenemunde-based rockets – struck by day. You stood little or no chance if you happened to be situated in their bulls-eye.

I knew how Mummy would be spending her time while I was at school. Proving herself a worthy recipient of all the benefits caring leaders had bestowed on the housewives of the nation. Making the very best of the allotted daily bread. It was cause for my constant amazement how she continued to put before us, day after day without fail, meals that were not only nourishing but varied and tasty. She herself was rightly proud of this – especially 'chuffed' about what she could do in what we dubbed 'lean week'. Rationing was structured by the month; for the first few days we would be feeling flush, but by the 21st or so things would definitely be 'lean' presenting a special challenge to all mothers to keep their broods well fed. Yet we never felt the slightest pinch, the slightest hint of 'I haven't had enough'. And moreover we never went short of a dessert: my favourite being Mother's tour de force; prosaically named 'grease pudding' it was sheer poetry to eat.

She several times threatened to write a book, 'Cooking with Rations'; doubtless it would have sold like her own hot cakes. What a pity she couldn't get around to it – too tied up with a myriad chores. Not only the cooking itself but looking after her second family: baby and toddler, stepfather too (I called him 'Step') and of course teenage me. It must be said, I never lent a hand, but I was never asked to. Had not Granddad declared, 'Iris needs to be waited on hand and foot' – how he had realised this, when I was a mere seven or eight, I don't know, but Mother seems to have gone along with it. Both granted that schoolwork, at which I excelled, gave me a certain licence.

'Labour saving devices' were at a premium then – in fact I think that's when this phrase was coined. Daily household routine included a longish walk to the shops and back for Mother with pram and toddler in tow, and more often than not plenty of queueing: sometimes for some rarely available item – not only imported 'luxuries' such as lemons but often sheer essentials too. Yet never once was my lunch not there for me when I darted in at 12:30 to wolf it down, along with wireless goodies such as 'Workers' Playtime'. Before rushing back for school at two.

Looking back decades from what is now largely a sedentary life, I'm struck by what a lot of walking I did, to and from school – four trips of nearly a mile each day. But never once did it tire me. I was no Roger Limbrey – but, ah, for the resilience of youth! Like so much else, you don't value it while you've got it, only after it's gone – presumably forever.

The Tracks

Only fairly recently have I come to realise that, strictly speaking, we were living on the wrong side of the tracks. The tracks being the railway itself – to be precise, the London North Eastern (LNER) that ran from Kings Cross to Edinburgh and points to the north and east. It's called something else now, but I guess the track itself the same, down to the very sleepers.

Before going any further, I must mention the Great Path Controversy. The footpath that ran alongside the LNER we at home called 'the railway path', while at school everyone called it 'the line path'. I was always on the defensive, always sticking up for the other usage – a trait I've observed in myself in other contexts. At home I'd defend 'line path' and at school vice-versa.

There was another example of differing usages – at home, when telling the time, we'd always say 'five-and-twenty to one' or 'five-and-twenty past two' whereas the kids invariably said 'twenty-five'. I asked a linguist friend about this. Was our version correct or theirs? And whence came the difference? Was it regional (Granddad hailed originally from Norfolk) or generational? She assured me 'generational' and I was gratified to find our version favoured by acceptably correct writers, not least Agatha Christie (always unfaultable language-wise).

By whatever name it's called, Roger Limbrey's trekking route was that path and I've no doubt it continues, in some form or other, to the left or right of the line, all the way to Scotland. Here and there it borders the Embankment – one of our favourite stamping grounds. That was quite a steep slope; you could roll down it and sometimes we did: not very advisable, but it was unlikely you'd end up on the line as, at its base, the Embankment had a little depression where you could come to rest (!) well below track level. And there were railings too.

We spent a lot of our leisure time on the Embankment, interspersing general fun with waving to the trains, always hoping to catch a glimpse of the undisputed favourite and super-celeb, The Flying Scotsman. We greatly appreciated it when the team on board waved back – as if acknowledging us as fans. The fireman and the guard, though not the driver of course – he had his job to concentrate on.

Once I experienced this waving thrill in reverse, on an adventurous spur-of-the-moment trip to Edinburgh. (It was my first foray 'abroad', i.e. outside England) – ostensibly for the Festival but really for an illicit rendezvous with a guy who happened to be taking part in it. I should point out that by this time I was no longer a kid but a budding, rash and particularly naïve teenager. A foolish virgin, let's say. However that may be, I got a big kick, as the train sped through Potters Bar, out of waving to my friends on the Embankment, not to mention identifying Rosemary's house. These sightings proved (in case I had ever doubted it) that my home-town Potters Bar was well and truly on the map – anyone going north or south by LNER had to pass through it and therefore be aware of its existence.

The Edinburgh trip, by the way, was far from being an unqualified success. My 'date' failed to turn up – probably his wife or his job stopped him – and I didn't see much of the Festival either. Not to mind! The exercise was worthwhile if only for a quip of Elsie's which it triggered. Going north, I'd shared a carriage with a Pole; coming south I'd equipped myself with a Swiss roll to stave off any possible hunger. Elsie summed it all up as follows, 'You went up with a Pole; you came back with a Swiss roll.'

***

Potters Bar's railway station was very near 301 – just beyond the blitzed homes of Ida and Ada. The station master, Mr Wilson, was one of Granddad's cronies; we regularly popped in at his office on our morning constitutionals – a week rarely passed without my seeing him. Yet, once when we met him by chance in another part of town, I didn't recognise him. I wondered, 'Who's this new friend of Granddad's?' The reason: he wasn't wearing his uniform – especially he was without his official hat! Not so odd after all when one reflects, who would recognise Nefertiti, or Yasser Arafat for that matter, without their distinctive headgear?

I thought of Mr Wilson vividly when, on 10th May 2002, the horrifying rail accident happened at Potters Bar. We saw on our TV screens half way across the world those so familiar scenes: the platforms, the waiting rooms, the station master's office – even the line of trees that can be seen from our garden at 301.

I visualised that particular stretch of the tracks where the disaster occurred: the part which is overlooked from the bridge in Mutton Lane and adjacent Bridge House, John Morris's home; it runs parallel to Stafford Gate where the Clefanes lived, with its own path accompanying the line as far as a second bridge, where the railway goes over the road, namely Darkes Lane. On that very sector of the line a carriage became detached from the rails and the whole train bore on its way, rising up terrifyingly, to land on a platform where passengers were waiting, and a sign reads 'Welcome to Potters Bar'. Several people were killed, including one who chanced to be walking along Darkes Lane under the bridge. Very often had I thought, as a youngster; *This place isn't safe; it's risky walking here as there's no pavement – you have to walk in the road.* I was picturing the danger as coming from traffic in the street, rather than from the trains above.

The lady who died there had lived in the town for about fifty years, that is approximately since the time I'd left it; I wondered if there had been a year or so of overlap between her sojourn and mine. The tragedy focused national attention; Prince Charles was among the first to rush with comfort and condolence to the nearest big hospital – the one in Enfield where the most serious cases from Potters Bar are transferred – indeed, Granddad breathed his last there. And it focused international attention too: for the memorial service world TV took us inside St Marys, The Walk, scene of Elsie's wedding, on Christmas Eve, 1933, at which I'd been part of the bridal group, a mite of three and a half.

Such are the many images and memories linked to 'The Tracks'. In my childhood and adolescence I never had any inkling of their social significance, but in later life I've come to see very clearly: we were very definitely on the wrong side of them and thus didn't belong, by a very long chalk, in the ranks of the élite – or even in those of the middle class per se. Rather, we were set four-square in the lower middle class – a very different kettle of fish. That isn't to say we weren't snobbish; in fact, of all the classes with which British society is riddled, none is more snobbery-prone than the lower middle. Envying those above, despising those below. For instance, some neighbours of ours, even stauncher Conservatives than we were, and loyally subscribing to the Daily Mail, viewed the folk living opposite them who took Labour's Daily Herald as well-nigh untouchables.

On the posh side of this definitive boundary – The Tracks – were some lovely leafy lanes – even leafier than those of Southgate. Beautiful houses too. Scoring points off Forestdale – no semi-detacheds here: yet another index of notches on the social scale. There were also some splendid gardens, notably that of Miss Blunt; Rosemary and I went to her every Saturday morning for elocution classes. She put us through our paces with Shakespeare and Wordsworth, preparing us to strut our stuff for an exam at the Poetry Society – I think we at least passed muster. I often thought: What a coincidence: Rosemary at Miss Blunt's, since of all Rosemary's defining qualities bluntness was one of the most outstanding. I would rarely if ever voice my views as frankly as she did. Together we would stroll along 'Blunt's Lane' as I called it – and it should be so named, I reckon, á la Darkes and Mutton – soaking up the privileged aura without, at our then tender age, soaking up its implications: 'These people have got a lot more money than we have' – or how unjust that was. But in due course Rosemary came to care passionately about such issues, striving in whatever way she could to 'build a new Jerusalem' – be it through, at first, politics, then, through her vocation with the Cooperative Society.

Yes, this was right side of the tracks all right, here in Blunt's Lane and allied avenues where Granddad's Bowling Club "bosses" tended to hang out. Super houses, super gardens. Yet I didn't complain about ours – few gardens anywhere could rival Granddad's for the care and knowledge he gave every seed he planted. And, to crown it all, he had an oak tree in pride of place. Not everyone, posh or other, can boast of that. I don't know when its acorn first got embedded but I do know that, after we left in 1950 shortly after Granddad died, the first act perpetrated by the new owners was to chop down the oak. They made other changes too that were far from enhancing. The walls of 301 had been embellished with myriads of little fawn and beige pebbles, giving the house a distinctive look – the newcomers made it their business to strip all these off and paint the walls a ghastly white, imparting to them the unnatural look of a clown, or a geisha.

If ever I regain possession of that, the dearest home I've ever had, I'll reverse those metamorphoses with a vengeance. I'll plant my own acorn in the very place where our oak stood so that it can start, asap, on its centuries-long growth to replace it. And I'll regain for the walls their old look. One change, however, I have to acknowledge as an improvement – I'd wanted to do it myself – that is, to install an extra room, as a study or den, in the 'loft' with doors leading from "my" room (erstwhile Mummy's too – Granddad had always let us have the upstairs front, i.e. the "masters") and that virginal sanctum of beloved Doris. This addition really does give an extra dimension and boy, would I make good use of it. No doubt some computer nerd is ensconced there now – but just wait till I regain my ancestral territory!

***

We seem to have travelled a long way from 'The Tracks'. A journey of self-recognition among other things. So we were lower middle class! A group neither loved nor admired by those above or below. Well, snobbery can hardly be expected to beget affection.

'Think you're posh, eh?' The council estate kids would taunt us.

'Yes, we are, so what?' would be our snooty riposte. 'Thank heaven we're not like you!' – flaunting my new Daniel Neale outfit for Easter Saturday – the chicest of the chic, the "little princesses" wouldn't be wearing better.

But this class divide didn't prevent me from having a friend or two among the council children. And, in a very real way, caring about them. Why should they have so much less than – never mind us but, say, the denizens of Blunt's Lane? And I was terribly upset when one of them, little Thelma of my own cohort, died of diphtheria. No immunisation against it then; she missed out on that by a few years.

The Tracks. What did they teach me? Well, sixty or seventy years on, I now know a bit more about class. Formidable though it be, it isn't the be all and end all. Sure, you should give it its due – take it into account, say, when choosing a mate. But, I repeat, it's not the be all and end all. There are more important entities that can knock it for six. Like say, friendship, or faith, or, even, let's face it, love.

I Don't Want to Set the World on Fire

No, but I very nearly did, once upon a time. For reasons unknown, and unknowable, once I found myself wandering as lonely as a cloud along the line/railway path towards Brookmans Park*. I didn't often go out alone.

Usually Marion, or a 'guild' member, or Rosemary (of course, accompanied by her mother) were with me. That day, however, I was devoid of fellow travellers.

Following the path almost as far as Roger Limbrey's cut-off point, the Embankment on my right (the Flying Scotsman had just whizzed past) I espied on my left a small spinney or copse. (Now it's probably high-rise or supermarket terrain). I crossed a demarcating fence and sauntered in. Fascinated. The flora and fauna in this place looked strikingly different from those in the open meadow bordering it.

Again, for some reason quite unknown, and unknowable, I thought it would be a good idea to start a fire. And so I did. I struck a match and almost immediately, in the clump of vegetation facing me, twigs ignited and started jerking about, all lit up. Fascinated again, this somehow made me see things in a different way. As different, say, as a movie is from a silent film. Doubtless alerted by these unfamiliarities, some woodland creatures scurried from their habitats into the relative safety of open space.

At first, the fire wasn't much more than embers. But they were spreading. Then – a sort of mini-rocket shot up out of the midst of them and landed in a neighbouring clump. And that really did catch fire – in earnest.

Suddenly I came to my senses. I was frightened. What had I done? Horrified, I began stamping on the flames – the new ones first – they were the more urgent – then the original ones. I didn't seem to be having much effect. Now I was

---

* Is there an apostrophe here or not? Or was there once and it's vanished, as in the case of Potter's Bar? – see piece on Charles Lamb

terrified – perhaps I couldn't put it out? What then? A bush fire, like in Australia? People might get killed. I might get killed. And so might any number of those innocent wood-dwellers – either killed or horribly hurt or maimed. 'Wee sleekit, cowerin', timorous beastie.' And it wasn't Robbie Burns doing this, accidentally – but me, intentionally.

Fortunately my frantic stampings at last began to work. The flames diminished, starting to sink down. I went over and over the two burning clumps. Yes, thank the Lord, they were indeed dying down. But again and again I went over them, checking and re-checking. Like an advanced case of obsessive compulsive disorder. Never mind that – never was compulsion more warranted. And sure enough, here and there, like an unstubbed-out fag, the odd spark lingered. More stamping. More and more. More checking, peering this way and that for the slightest remaining residue.

At last, at very long last, I was satisfied – all was perfectly quenched, bone dry. Only then could I stop my manic manoeuvres – and, eventually, go home. With a hard-won clear conscience. But perturbed, nonetheless. How on earth could I have done that? Why, for Pete's sake?

I still don't know. But what I do see is – I'd failed to differentiate between what had appealed to my imagination, and the real thing: the mental picture of a fire as opposed to what would actually happen once I struck a match. For me there had always been a blurred grey area between the imagined and the real – but, up till then, it hadn't mattered much. It had been purely theoretical. What happened in the wood that day was anything but. All this was a lesson to me delivered none too soon to see things as they really are.

I was about eight or nine. Well past the 'age of reason' as defined by some. I'm not so sure. I thought of a terrible crime perpetrated by two boys of ten – killing a toddler. You can't get inside the heads of such youngsters – or indeed of anyone when it comes to the crunch. It seemed they just didn't comprehend the enormity of what they had done – till it was far too late, when one of them said, 'What about his mum? Tell her I'm sorry.' The truth had at last got through to him. Maybe for those two it had been a sort of ghastly 'playgame'. At any rate, a game, not for real. After all, football isn't real – it's sheer pretend, make believe. What is Manchester United? It doesn't really hate Arsenal, or Chelsea or Barca, or whatever – they just want to beat the living daylights out of each other.

Fortunately I'd realised in time the truth about what I was doing. *Deo gratias.*

As to how I did it – another conundrum. I wasn't in the habit of carrying matches – what would I have needed them for? I didn't smoke – for heaven's sake. And although our "guild" had some weird stipulations, matches didn't figure in any of them, and I'm sure I wouldn't have been able to perform the famous Boy Scouts tour de force – rubbing two sticks together – even if I'd studied it, which I hadn't. I'd always shied away from set-ups like Scouts and Guides, geared as they are to practical goings-on, which I'd always found off-putting. "Iris isn't practical" – one of Mother's verdicts on me, most of which were bang on target. I was a very slow and unwilling learner when it came to things like that. But I reckon I should have been forced to learn them, whether I liked it or not. So should all kids. Either in school or in Scouts or whatever – all the so-useful and especially life-saving actions. Not only how to start a fire, and how to put it out. How to swim. Drive a car. Give first aid. An initiation everyone should go through before being accepted as an adult. A celebration laid on to provide incentive. Like, say, a bar mitzbah.

We simply weren't taught such things. Some were available – like swimming classes, but some kids like me could eschew them if they felt so inclined. Instead, what was forced down our throats was algebra and trigonometry and, yes, Robbie Burns – all very well, but hardly life-savers.

I see I was allowed, with the best intentions in the world, to go my own sweet way, with excessive freedom to indulge my whims. What should really be 'eschewed' is too much freedom.

Here endeth the lesson. Or perhaps I should say 'Here beginneth'.

Der Old Vic

The war wasn't all unmitigated misery; in fact, large chunks of it were enjoyable. None more so than the wireless programmes we looked forward to eagerly each week. One of them began like this:

It's Monday night at eight o'clock
Oh, can't you hear The Chimes?*
They're telling you to take an easy chair
To settle by the fireside, get out your Radio Times,
For 'Monday Night at Eight' is on the air.

    This was followed by another verse outlining what was being offered for our delectation that particular evening.

    Among the regular performers in 'Monday Night at Eight' was Sarah Churchill, daughter of the Prime Minister. She was married to a prominent comedian, Vic Oliver; the Churchill family probably weren't very keen on that but they had no choice but to lump it.

    As for the rest of us, it suited us fine. Vic was a top-favourite radio personality. He was doing his very big bit, not unworthy of his father-in-law, to keep our spirits up in those dark times. Not only was he a first-rate comedian; he was also a violinist of distinction and often included a violin solo in his act. The clown playing Hamlet? Well, why not, when he plays it supremely well? He was wont to refer to himself a 'Der Old Vic' and never modified his foreign accent or disguised the fact that he hailed from central Europe. Perhaps he was Jewish too – that was neither here nor there.

---

* The girl vocalists were called "The Three Chimes".

He was also a mainstay of another weekly 'must hear', namely *Hi, Gang!* co-starring with Bebe Daniels and Ben Lyon. This was second only to *ITMA* (*It's That Man Again*) – undoubtedly the show of the war; nothing short of a national institution – to the extent that its star, Tommy Handley, was laid to rest in St Paul's Cathedral.

Missing out on *Itma* or *Hi, Gang!* or *Monday Night at Eight* would spoil one's entire week; we were absolutely in thrall to our wireless sets, surmounted in millions of homes by a photo of Mr Churchill. He was just plain 'Mister' throughout the war; afterwards, the most he made it to, or would accept, was 'Sir'. No peerage for him, though nowadays they are bestowed ten-a-penny on mediocrities.

When Sarah had finished her broadcast she'd make her way home through the blacked-out city – maybe to the flat she shared with Vic or maybe to No. 10, like Dad. But not all the cast of *Monday Night at Eight* made it safely through the bombarded streets; there was a whodunit slot in the show and its sleuth, Inspector Hornsleigh, perished in an air raid. The Blitz was no respecter of celebrity.

Apart from radio (of course, no TV then) Vic played the 'West End' and I well recall seeing him in *Starlight Roof*. As a treat for my passing 'matric' (dread hurdle between school and university) one of Doris's glamorous friends, Lalla Scruby, took me, with Doris, to a show of my choosing. What other choice could there possibly be when Vic was on offer?

His lines were very witty and a shade risqué. This no doubt encouraged me and a close friend of those days – whom I'll call Madge Smythe – to write him a begging letter. I must stress that neither Madge nor I breathed a word of this to our families. Granddad and Doris would have been horrified; I didn't even dare tell Elsie – though I could have told Mummy about it. She was by far the least conventional of the three sisters; she'd identify with the cheek and chutzpah involved – an escapade akin to her own high jinks re Brian Lawrence.

By this time Madge and I were working – though we were barely more than children, (me 16, she 15), earning our living, i.e. slaving away for a pittance at Harrods, in their Book Department and Library (pre-Fayed, of course; maybe he pays better). So we were chronically hard-up. We felt that all the more because all London had been set before us and we wanted to savour to the utmost its countless delights, but most were beyond our means. Further, we had developed expensive tastes such as eating in Italian Soho restaurants. So we thought – why not the begging letter? What have we got to lose?

Accordingly, we drew up a list of ten "victims". They included Vic Oliver and the King – these are the only names I remember, must be because they were the only ones who answered. Though neither sent any money, both replies were surprisingly not unsympathetic – politely regretful but uncensorious. Vic's naturally was much less formal, ending with a sly PS, 'Do I know you?'

Another quiver to his bow was that he ran a weekly talent-spotting series this too on radio. I would rush home at lunch time even faster than usual to catch it. For quite a few years there had been a husband-and-wife variety team, Ted and Barbara Andrews, often featuring in, among others, *Workers' Playtime*, aired to coincide with factory lunch breaks. I liked their act, as well as their signature tune, 'I'll get by/as long as I/have you.' Their thirteen-year-old daughter was aspiring to be a singer and Vic gave her a chance on his programme. She sang 'One Fine Day'. Her name was Julie Andrews.

In the course of time he and Sarah split up and he remarried. The latter years of his life were full of family happiness, which he assuredly deserved. He didn't retire, though. He died on duty, on tour in Johannesburg, in his dressing room. For one who was such a quintessential man of the theatre, what more fitting end?

Field Day

It must have started around late afternoon and lasted well into the evening – this was still pre-war, so there was no air-raid menace. At any rate, there were hours of it, hours of undiluted pleasure, non-stop. We were having a whale of a time. But what were we actually doing? I'd be hard-pressed to say. I suppose – just being there. A group of us – not the 'guild', which had already fizzled out. Merely a random batch of classmates and neighbours.

It all took place in a field. No ordinary field this – never seen the likes of it before or since. Nothing special to look at, but special in no small measure. Irregularly shaped, roughly triangular bordered on one side by a big hedge – a row of bushes and shrubs. A three-dimensional hedge, you might say, consisting of a series of small enclosures, like little caves. Beyond this boundary lay another, very different kind of field, wide open territory where bulls were monarchs of all they surveyed, especially cows but possibly us too if we ventured too close. No doubt about it, that bordering hedge certainly served a useful purpose!

On the second side of the field was the railway/line path and the Embankment and on the third the streets of an estate of which Rosemary's house stood at the very end, right next to "our" field which was in a sense her extended garden. That was doubtless why her mother hadn't chosen to accompany her on this escapade – she could easily view what was going on from an upstairs window.

The field was overgrown and downright neglected, left to its own devices for a long time. In fact it looked as if it hadn't been tended or cultivated for ages. It wasn't a matter of lying fallow, rather left to run wild indefinitely. Unlike the hedge, it wasn't serving a useful purpose – except unintentionally as a playground for kids like us. And no ordinary playground at that.

Its most interesting aspect was certainly that hedge, with its series of small enclosures; veritable mini-caves, naturally evolved shelters as it were, each with its own 'entrance' and 'walls'. Each about the size and shape of a smallish igloo. And indeed it could be a tiny home. But for whom? No Inuit around here! Tramps, possibly? The sort of people who sleep rough, whether by choice or necessity – on pavements, in cardboard boxes. To such as those this might seem a cosy refuge indeed. What about immigrants? But of course, there weren't any of them those days. Gypsies maybe – there were quite a lot of those, always have been. But so far no one at all had taken up residence here.

We delved into the potential dwellings one by one, exploring them, seeing what they had to offer us. A sprig or two of flowering shrub; a field mouse – we wrapped him up tenderly to take him home as a new pet.

It wasn't only the hedge that drew us; the field had other attractive features. There was a stream running through it – probably had been since Domesday times – indeed all this is just a stone's throw from Wyllyott's Manor.

Time passed. Hours went by unnoticed. More exploring. Collecting odd bits and pieces. Such as various curiously shaped stones. And doing what amounted to – nothing in particular. Talk about *dolce far niente*! But sometimes that is the most positive thing you can do. At the very least, it does serve to recharge one's batteries. And you couldn't get more fun out of listening to TV for hours – or even the wireless.

About half-way through this happening we saw another group of kids approaching, climbing over the railings on the Embankment side. Intruders! Invaders! Should we engage in battle? After a brief consultation we came up with the decision, 'No. What for?' Anyway, we didn't have any weapons (of mass destruction or other). 'Live and let live!' The field was quite big enough for all comers – with, perhaps, a few exceptions. A hostile element might just try to get in…We should at any rate equip ourselves, perhaps acquire an arsenal of sticks and stones ("rocks" as the Americans call them) for use against any possible assailants who might be similarly armed. And keep our ammunition in a special place – one of the caves would do.

Time continued to pass and it began to get dark. We were beginning to feel tired. And beginning to think 'Enough is enough'. Better call it a day – albeit a field day. Time to go home. When we got there we were in fact thoroughly exhausted. And thoroughly dirty too. Like rugby players after their scrums – in need of a jolly good bath.

Luckily it was Friday – bath night. Those were the days when a weekly bath was the norm. None of your daily shower stuff then! We had boilers that used a special fuel – coke (and I don't mean Coca Cola). That whole operation was taken care of by Granddad – providing a plenteous supply of piping hot water. It was traditionally shampoo night too – as a current slogan put it, 'Friday night is Amami night', plugging a well known make: Betjeman countered it for a rival firm, describing how young ladies of a Friday night delicately drown in Drene.

'Those were the days, my friend…' or rather, the day. The day, I should say, 'cos there was never another quite like it. And we never attempted to repeat it – I wonder why. Perhaps we realised, its magic couldn't be recaptured. Magic rarely can. Or – more prosaically – perhaps because our families were a bit cross – and/or worried. Used to so much freedom as we were, we had nonetheless overstepped the mark; got a bit filthier, stayed out a bit later, than was permissible/acceptable. So, ever so mildly, they put their foot down.

By the way, the field mouse didn't survive more than a few hours.

Despite our so well-intentioned 'care'. It wasn't a field day for him.

Gas

'Mussolini has used gas on the Abyssinians.'

Granddad made this announcement as he came in through the kitchen door one evening in 1935.

Like everyone who had lived through WWI, for him the horror of gas used in warfare could never be forgotten. Even without Wilfred Owen's poem, *Dulce et Decorum*, everyone knew. And in the 1930s, the WWI years were quite recent past. Their events were still fresh in people's minds.

Awareness of those horrors was transmitted to us of a younger generation, firstly by word of mouth, and then through the informative material we were issued relevant to incipient WWII and what might reasonably be expected to be inflicted on us. It was thought more than likely that Hitler would use this terrible weapon like the Kaiser before him. Hence the commendable speed of measures to equip us all with gas masks. Even the need of babies for a special kind, made more acceptable by embellishment with Walt Disney images, was thought of and provided. Everyone was tested, as early as the Munich crisis – no waiting till war actually broke out. Granny and I went to be 'done' at Wyllyotts Manor, which by then had become the administrative hub of Potters Bar.

In the informative leaflets, mustard gas and phosgene were specifically mentioned, and we were briefed about the rattles that would serve as warning of an imminent attack. Thank God we never heard them! It was my constant prayer that we never would and the prayer was answered. *Deo gratias*.

The fear of gas, I can truly say, was the greatest fear besetting my childhood. There weren't many – again, *Deo gratias*. I wasn't yet aware of so many of the dreadful things that human beings – and animals – can fall victim to. I found out about some of them years later, partly though my decades-long work with WHO; such knowledge hardly enhanced my peace of mind.

"When ignorance is bliss

'Tis folly to be wise."

I can't argue with that.

Gas. And there was another form of it, albeit relatively benign, that nonetheless triggered panicky feelings in me. The so-called 'laughing gas', commonly used then at dentists' for procedures such as extractions and root canal work, which otherwise would be agonising. It carried the same risk as all general anaesthesia – the possibility of not coming around. Plus – patients were reputed to babble under it, maybe broadcasting to the rooftops things they wished desperately to keep to themselves – as I've mentioned in the piece referring to my secret but very real passion for Pat Garland. (See 'Three Wartime Heroes.')

Gas. It isn't a word to feel comfortable with. And now, so much later on, it has additional connotations: Sylvia Plath and others who chose to make their exit from this life by such means.

Gas. When I catch sight of this word – in whatever context, standing alone or perhaps in a crossword puzzle – it arouses in me very unquiet feelings. And always will, I reckon.

Apart from that, I shall never forget Granddad coming in through the kitchen door that evening in 1935 and telling us that chilling news, which had obviously disturbed him deeply. 'Mussolini has used gas on the Abyssinians.' I can still see his distressed expression: it was a very accurate reflection of his feelings. He cared about what happened to those Abyssinians. Remote though they were, living on another continent, on the wrong side of the 'colour bar' we heard a lot about those days and which, it must be admitted, many Brits condoned, lumping all non-whites together as 'lesser breeds without the law'. But not Granddad. He cared. About the suffering of any living creature. He was among the very best of Brits.

Sandbags or Money Bags?

Everyone had to do something for the war effort. Every single home – including of course 301 Mutton Lane, identity-labelled BNAN 161 (of which I was BNAN 161 5, being the littlest of the originally five-member household).

It wasn't so much an order as an axiom – no one questioned it. We assumed 'everyone' included kids – at any rate, we Cranbornites wanted to do our bit not one whit less than the grown-ups. We asked our immediate ARP group for a job and, a shade puzzled, they suggested, 'Perhaps you could fill some sandbags?'

By all means! And we set to with a will. But it was hard work. Back-breaking! I couldn't keep it up for very long. Some of my ex-guild mates accused me that the sum total of my war effort amounted to one filled sandbag.

Not so! Because, unbeknownst to them, I had another string to my patriotic bow. Collecting money. To buy bombs, 'hopefully' to shower on the 'Huns' (no political correctness then!) Unlike Mr Bath, I didn't have the slightest compunction about showering as many bombs as possible on them, since they'd been doing that to us non-stop for months.

So I set off on my fund-raising way, optimistically equipped with a big collecting tin such as carol singers brandish, or ladies selling flags for people's lapels on Queen Alexandra's Nurses' Day. (In the high summer Mummy and most of her glamorous friends did this). Instinctively I headed for the posher parts of town, well and truly on the right side of the tracks and for good measure on the far side of the golf links too. You can't get much posher than that in the confines of Potters Bar. Surely in such affluent hunting grounds one could expect to bag enough to arm a sizeable fleet of Spitfires and Hurricanes! Not necessarily – as I soon found out.

The first household I decided to pester was one that easily outdid the best des-res. displayed in 'Ideal Homes'. Called 'Silver Abbey', it was more than impressive – a beautiful façade and fabulous grounds (no mere garden this). Granddad would have been in his utmost element there; though he would have needed a whole bevy of monks to run all those lawns and flower beds. Did people actually live in places like this? They might be real estate – but were they real? Were they even liveable in? Apparently, yes. Not bloody likely though that folk like us would ever be so accommodated – or even feel comfortable if we were. Talk about 'The Flowers are not for You to Pick', talk about 'beyond your station'. Buckingham Palace itself would have felt more 'homey'.

Nevertheless, undaunted I firmly knocked on the knocker of Silver Abbey. Appropriately enough it was cast in the mould of King Richard Coeur de Lion. Confident that at least I'd get a civil response to my civil request. Again, not so. The lady who opened the door at once silenced me with – believe it or not,

'I will give you nothing for weapons of mass destruction.'

Hans Blix should have been around! Perhaps he was – a ghost from the then distant future.

Door slammed in my face, undeterred I went on my way. Braving scores of similar right-royal knockers. But to my surprise and delight, all these other 'pesterees' coughed up generously. In an incredibly short time my tin was quite heavy – a lot heavier in fact than my piggy bank when I'd been saving up long-term – and it clanked very satisfyingly. At least I'd managed to garner in more than the average carol singing group on a good night. Perhaps not enough to arm a Hurricane or Spitfire but maybe it might suffice for a bayonet or two. I felt a bit smug – self-righteous, even. Little ten-year-old me, a.k.a. BNAN 161 5, hadn't let Mr Churchill down!

I can't recall who I had to hand it all over to. Mr Sims probably, or Mr Gascoigne – Head and form master respectively. Very trusting of them – I could have pocketed the lot!

Evacuees

Anyone contemplating the outbreak of WWII, even long before it started, would have visualised two inevitable aspects: air raids and civilian casualties. On a scale so far unknown – previous wars, 'World' and other, had mainly taken toll of the military. Plans had to be made quickly to minimise what is now so heartlessly referred to as 'collateral damage'.

It was realised that most residents of target areas couldn't leave; those in jobs had to go on working; others had to 'keep the home fires burning'. All these would have to stay put and take their chance. Adults, that is. Children were a different matter. Evacuating them to safer areas was just doable and the government took prompt steps towards doing it. Many thousands of people all over the country were only too keen to take in these little home-grown refugees – and that's what happened, on quite a large scale. In addition, several friendly countries offered asylum to an unlimited number of British children; plans for that, too, were well under way by the time war started. We in Potters Bar being in the banlieu, so to speak, of London the prime target, were naturally among the most eligible for evacuation. As early as the phoney war stage, our families were given a choice: where would you like your little ones to go? Canada, Australia, New Zealand, USA? Like all my friends, I myself was allowed to choose, and I plumped for Canada – why, I haven't the slightest idea.

Even then, and even more so now, I marvelled that I wasn't filled with dread at the very thought of leaving. Going thousands of miles away to live with complete strangers. In a completely strange country. Leaving home! Leaving 301! And everyone in it! Not knowing when, or indeed if, I should ever see them again. Granny and Granddad were well into their sixties – and who knew how long the war would last? Maybe longer than WWI's four years. And what sort of fate would befall me in that distant place? Most of all, how would I deal with the actual day of departure – which, we knew, couldn't be very far ahead. Would I go calmly – or have to be dragged, screaming…? True, all these thoughts were in my mind, but strangely, they had no impact on my emotions, which I kept firmly switched off. I suppose I just didn't dare have them switched on. 'Defence mechanism', shrinks might well say.

In the meantime we went ahead with the nitty-gritty. Such as getting warm clothing. Also, Mother felt she must brief me about the 'facts of life'. Including about menarche. Pointing out, 'This is pretty sure to happen to you when you're in Canada.' I was appalled. I'd had no inkling of that biological phenomenon – a messy and possibly painful ordeal to face every month. How on earth would I cope? 'You'll cope,' Mother assured me. 'Everyone does.'

'Does everyone have to go through it?' was my desperate query. Hoping against hope. 'Aren't there any exceptions?'

Taking pity on me, Mother conceded, white-lie-style, 'Well, maybe the odd freak here and there.' I ardently hoped I'd be one of the odd freaks.

So, plans were proceeding inexorably, denial was continuing unabated, the date of severance relentlessly approaching. But – it didn't happen. The whole plan was suddenly scrapped – because the Germans sank a merchant ship, the Arandora Star, with many civilians aboard. So – no Canada, here we don't come. I ought to have heaved a sigh of relief, but didn't – not consciously at any rate; in denial as I was, there' d have been no raison d'être for that. However, I'm certain that everyone else at 301 offered up prayers of thanksgiving that their little 'Timmy' wasn't going to be wrenched away from them. Granny, Granddad, Doris, Mummy – the entire BNAN 161 household. I'm certain the separation would have been even worse for them than for me – 'cos, no doubt about it, they loved me yeah, yeah, yeah.

This overseas avenue closed, schemes for local evacuation were stepped up. Again, Marion and I were top eligibles, and allotted a proposed destination. This time there was no choice – it was Newquay in Cornwall. A place deemed about as safe as you could get on these islands, certainly not in a target area, although some big cities in neighbouring Devon – Plymouth and Exeter – received their own specially devised and specially savage Blitz nights. Such visitations were known as 'Baedeker' raids – named after a well-known tourist guide book, aimed at cultural centres so as to puncture our morale.

Unlike Canada, the Newquay prospect filled me with pleasure and excitement. It wouldn't involve a traumatic separation. We wouldn't be cut off from our families; probably they could visit us from time to time. Moreover, we'd be going to a place known to be a delightful holiday resort. In fact, a treat was being handed us on a plate. We fantasised about 'N' as we called it, as we cuddled each other in Marion's bed – during one such cuddle the landmine fell on the cemetery less than mile up Mutton Lane.

But this plan too never got off the ground. I don't know why. Perhaps because of arrangements about schools or billeting? Anyway, the outcome was – we too just stayed where were and took our chance like the grown-ups.

Plenty of other kids, though, throughout Britain, were successfully lodged with volunteer hosts in what was deemed safe territory. 'Evacuees' as they were called became one of those distinct segments of the population peculiar to wartime – like, say, 'landgirls' or 'conchies'. We met one of them, a boy from central London, staying with friends of Doris in the Hertfordshire outback – to wit, a little town called Boxmoor. It was quite a trek to get there, via St Albans and Hemel Hempstead; Doris loved such excursions and loved too to take me with her. It was good to see the little Londoner settled in so happily with these good, caring people. And to know that there were thousands of such arrangements flourishing all over the land. The authorities had chosen Boxmoor well as it was far enough from a Luftwaffe target, Baedeker or other. And also just beyond the range of the V2 rockets fired from Holland – though no one could have known about those at that earlier stage of the war. Serendipitous let's call it.

So we stayed put, until, as the ferocious endgame of WWII was entered, these same V2s, not to mention V1s, started to drop on our native heath, whether Potters Bar or Southgate. Regarding the V1s, the mental anguish of hearing those 'pilotless planes' chug-chug, chug-chug, which would suddenly stop and then you'd know the thing was about to drop – landing where was anyone's guess. As for the V2s, there was no preliminary sound; they just arrived, and exploded, any time (usually during the day), any place. You could be out shopping for instance – not a thing you could do to take refuge. This was stress that proved too much for many, including Mummy who so far had withstood all the other pressures of war. Worry about her children was the main factor; it must not be forgotten that she wasn't all that strong, psychologically, with her case history of mental disorder. I think she was on the verge of cracking, and might have had to be hospitalised again. She herself probably felt she was at risk of that.

However that may be, for a very brief period we ourselves became 'evacuees'. We went north, to stay with my aunt Elsie who was then living in Ormskirk, Lancashire, between Liverpool and Preston, but quite far from both cities which were bombable but far beyond the range of V1s and 2s. I could see Blackpool Tower from my bedroom window there. This trip was like going 'abroad' – to an area very different from my native southern England. Lancashire is very different and nothing marks this more than its characteristic black earth.

One day Elsie's husband, Uncle Jack, took me and their daughter, together with a New Zealand friend, on a long walk in the surrounding countryside. Up a steep hill to a place called The Devil's Wall. On the way we passed several lorry-loads of prisoners of war (another category of wartime personnel), Italian prisoners of war at that. Did I sit up and take notice! What attractive creatures! Little "Timmy" was beginning to grow up. I had already fallen in love with Italy, and everything Italian, Roman, or Latin (via Ruth's collection of operatic discs) and the sighting of these prisoners did nothing to reverse that trend.

We went on along the Wall to a point where, lo and behold, suddenly a stunning panoramic view was spread out before us. You could see right across Liverpool, protected as it was by a 'ceiling' of balloon barrage, to Wales in the far distance. Little did we know then that somewhere down there in the great city must have been four toddlers, destined eventually to take the world by storm. No prizes for guessing their names. Only, at that point, Yoko wasn't yet there – unlike Mr Fujihito of Forestdale, electing to stay in her native land till the time was right, and ripe, for her to enact her famous legend.

We didn't stay very long in the North. Duty called us back to London, where both Daddy and Step were sticking it out, unable to leave their jobs. Exposed non-stop to Luftwaffe, V1s, V2s – the lot. In fact Step had been injured in the course of his (dangerous) wartime work in a foundry – not too seriously, praise be.

And praise be, too, in a matter of a few months, the war was over. In Europe that is, and it was time for hard-earned VE celebrations. Dancing in the streets, no less. And, not the least cause for joy, for 'evacuees' to return home – provided, of course, they had a home to return to.

Natushka

It's very rarely, if ever, mentioned in war reports how many animals were killed or injured in this or that incident. Air raids, for instance. Even in U.K., notoriously animal-loving nation – though non-human victims there probably greatly outnumbered human ones: it's as if they didn't matter.

We as a family became acutely aware of this because of Natushka.

My mother found this little cat, scarcely more than a kitten, lying on the Verge outside our gate, wounded by shrapnel from the previous night's bombing. Mother happened to know who the owners were – and they proved to be far from 'notoriously animal loving'. When shown the little creature's condition and need for treatment their response was,

'Why not put it out with a brick?'

Mother's answer to that was,

'If that's your attitude then I'll take care of her – but she'll be mine from now on.'

And so she was. Mother nursed her back to good shape – better surely than she'd ever been before – at the same time providing her with a secure, loving home which she was to enjoy for many years to come – at Mutton Lane and later when Mother, Step and their new family set up home in Southgate and subsequent abodes. And it was I incidentally who chose that name for her, 'Natushka'.

'A cat and dog life' – a myth if ever there was one. Natushka and Bob Rodwell, and later his successor little daschund Humfri, got on absolutely fine together. Part of our household every bit as much as we humans. In fact I reckon the government ought to have allocated each one of them a BNAN 161 identity number.

The Cloudburst

'An Englishman's home is his castle.' This applied to Granddad as much as to any of his compatriots. But when it came to The Cloudburst, the portcullis was let down in a big way. I'll explain.

As mentioned above, 301 together with its semi-detached neighbour, Marion's home, was located immediately opposite the bus-stop where a queue was to be seen throughout each day, throughout each year, waiting for the London-bound No. 29. (And also the 313 from St Albans, though that was a less frequent caller.) The 29 on its longest haul could take us from South Mimms to Victoria and back, so Piccadilly and Leicester Square were to all intents and purposes on our doorstep.

Looking out from our front room (the 'lounge' as we called it) we came to know a lot of queuers by sight, by virtue of their standing patiently there day after day, year in year out. We got to know the names of a few of them through mutual acquaintances rather than by speaking directly. Among these were Ada and Ida, those maiden ladies who fell victim to the Blitz – the direct hit on their home in Laurel Avenue which links our part of Mutton Lane with the railway station: that was the nearest the bombs came to us, a stone's throw or two. Another queuer known by name was Audrey Smith, a few years my senior, commuting to her secondary school, Minchenden, some miles off in Greater London – fierce rival of Southgate County School, my father's alma mater where I was eventually enrolled. Derek Stockbridge too became a Minchendenite – thus we were launched on separate (confrontational – Eton and Harrow were hardly more so) – paths after the crucial eleven-plus exam. Rosemary went on to yet another select establishment, Barnet's Queen Elizabeth's School for Girls – (no co-ednonsense there). I don't know where John Morris, the fourth of our famous foursome, was syphoned off to, but it must have been somewhere of comparable calibre; Potters Bar was in the catchment area of several of what used to be called grammar schools, where the bright kids were sent and where the secondary education was, in those days, the best Britain has ever offered.

If we rarely spoke to those people of the queue, even when standing in line with them, much less did we ever invite them in. Ours was a silent camaraderie – but a camaraderie nonetheless. Something of a shared 'grinning and bearing' about it – queueing acknowledged by all to be one of the banes of life in U.K. – surpassed only by the weather, or the war when that was part of the environment. But some individuals – masochists, what else? – regarded it as a sort of pastime!

No, we didn't open up easily to each other, albeit subject to a shared plight. Such is Brit reserve – stiff upper lip and all that. Things are different in the North Country, and the West Country, Scotland and even the Midlands. But London and the Home Counties are a law unto themselves. Their typical attitude I was amused to find reflected in an Arabic proverb I came across many years later in Egypt:

Sabah el kheir, ya gari
Good morning, my neighbour
Inta fi khálak, we ana fi kháli

You mind your own business, and I mind mine.

So – an Egyptian's home is his castle too – or should I say his pyramid? But come The Cloudburst – and all that reserve went by the board!

'What's a cloudburst?' you might be asking. Well, it's just that – a cloud simply bursts and empties its entire contents right on top of where you're standing, including right on top of your head.

This happened late one afternoon to a string of queuers at our stop. The heavens had opened and these folk were on the receiving end. At once Granddad signalled to them, 'Come on in!' And they did – some half dozen or so total strangers. No regulars, known by name or sight, among them; all extremely glad of the providential respite afforded by 301. We all stood around chatting in our 'hall' while Mummy plied them with tea. For almost an hour they stayed. No sign of the bus; usually it came every few minutes but it too seemed unable to struggle through the sheer volume of water. Even if it could have done so, our queuer guests would hardly have been able to reach it, wading through the virtual 'moat' the 'castle' had acquired. Someone said, 'Maybe Noah's flood started like this.' Maybe. The difference being, his didn't stop for a very long time.

Mercifully, eventually, ours did. Eventually, blessedly, there it was – the red double decker valiantly appearing over the crest of the hill in the middle distance.

A big cheer went up. Crisis passed! Our erstwhile visitors could now venture on their way. Ships that pass in the night indeed. Or rather in the late afternoon.

We never saw any of them again – or I don't think we did. But if we had bumped into any of them on, say, the Costa Brava or some ski lift in Switzerland, we'd hardly have recognised each other, would we?

I was going to call this piece 'How to have fun though drenched' but that would have been inaccurate. I was the one thoroughly enjoying it all; they were the drenched ones. However, I do like to hope they look back with pleasure, and warmth, on their brief, providential and totally unexpected visit to 'an Englishman's castle'. They might even remember it all their lives.

The Edith Duckett Story

John Steinbeck recounts in his 'Notebooks' how his father had told him things that, then, were known to no other person. When the father died, therefore, they were known only to Steinbeck and, if he kept them to himself, would be lost forever. He thus saw it as his duty to publish them – so now the whole world knows about them, instead of no one.

A strikingly similar situation prevailed in my family. My mother had many, many times told me the story of Edith Duckett. It was a tale, a horrifyingly true tale, that had had a profound and lasting effect on her. And it impressed me too, even when I first heard it as a child. It is a moving story by any standard.

It took place when my mother was fifteen, in the middle of WWI. In Gathorne Road, Wood Green, the Ducketts were our (the Rodwells') next-door neighbours and at Wood Green County School, Edith was Mama's classmate and bosom friend. They couldn't have been closer. They confided everything in each other. Such as – the boys they had strong feelings for, whether requited or not.

One day Edith fell ill. Her mother called my grandmother to come and look at her. They got doctors – but to no avail. By the next day she was gone. Suspicion fell on something eaten; they had had game for dinner – pheasant. No one else suffered any ill effect – except the cat, who died. It was assumed that gunshot had been left in the flesh of the bird. This must have been verified at autopsy.

Surrounded by the devastations of war in the trenches, even so this domestic disaster struck home to my mother as the most catastrophic blow of all. The sheer shock of it. The closeness. Poignantly she told me of the funeral – most poignant of all was how, standing by Edith's graveside, was that boy she'd so intensely set her heart on.

This tragedy played itself over and over in Mother's memory. She even spoke to me about it when, in 1956, I visited her in England – when I saw her for the last time.

The Great War continued, with the horrors of Flanders, the Somme, Ypres and Passchendaele leaving their mark on Gathorne Road and Wood Green as on the rest of the nation. Every now and then a soldier was granted compassionate leave from the front line when there was an even more pressing trauma taking place at home. The names of some Gathorne neighbours ring on in my memory, relayed to me by the older generation, their contemporaries; they linger on, right into this the twenty-first century. The name of Kate Sparshott living a few doors along, is one of those unforgettables; so is Mr Whitworth, the English teacher living opposite. I wonder if anyone else knows about those people now.

And after the fighting ended, suffering didn't. Another calamity struck world-wide, claiming even more casualties than the war – the flu pandemic. And our little street wasn't immune to that either. Gladys Hawkey, another close neighbour, succumbed in 1919 – having gone through WWI unscathed. Her mother too called Granny – to her lying in state. She told her, 'Poor darling, all her life she was so unhappy about her nose, she felt it wasn't pretty, a real handicap. But look! Now, after passing away, miraculously it seems, it has become beautiful.'

Diana Garrod

Diana has long been a favourite name of mine, long, long before Lady Di appeared on our horizons, or was even born. And I've encountered no more inspiring example of it than Diana Garrod – one of my 'most memorable teachers'. I liked her surname, too, and I liked her.

She took us in the middle juniors at Cranborne, the year before Mr Bath. What was so striking about her? Several things. Firstly, her looks. She was a splendid creature, a real joy to look at, especially when she was angry – which, understandably, was quite often: we kids played her up. But we didn't dare do too much of that, because she was no disbeliever in corporal punishment. If my memory serves me right, once she gave me a swipe across the palm. With a ruler, was it? Or her bare hand? If the latter, it must have hurt her too. And for what misdemeanour? 'Talking', again, most probably – the cardinal sin of kids in class. I don't blame teachers for resorting to mild force – you've got to discipline the brats somehow, and get some knowledge into their heads. But 'violence' as such was out of her character. Way out. She was fundamentally gentle and kindly.

But back to her looks. She wouldn't have let Diana the huntress down. Her marvellous crown of golden loosely curled hair was especially splendid.

I don't remember her teaching as such. It must have been all right though, as we passed all the tests and progressed satisfactorily. And I must have done rather well, because at the end of the school year she announced a treat for the top two in the form. These happened to be me and Margaret Wood; that was noteworthy since, apart from that year, right through the school Rosemary and I always shared the top slots, either she first and me second or vice-versa, Margaret running us a very close third. That year perhaps Rosemary had been absent at test time, off sick maybe?

Anyway, Diana Garrod bestowed the reward on me and Margaret – a lovely classmate; I wish I had been closer to her, got to know her better. But my supreme bond with Rosemary tended to preclude other close friendships.

The treat was a trip to Whipsnade, the open zoo in the countryside not far away, where elephants, giraffes, zebras et al roamed freely, safari-style. With a crony of hers for company, Diana took us by car. She drove. Having a car at all, not to mention driving it, was unusual then, something to write home about. In those days only the comparatively affluent – like dear Uncle Sid had been before the war put a stop to his promising stockbroker career – could afford such luxuries.

I thoroughly enjoyed the treat. Not the least of its satisfactions was that I went through the whole day without need of or recourse to toilets, for either big or little jobs. I had determined, on setting out, that I would do that and I was able to fulfil my 'commitment'.

In fact, throughout my entire Cranborne life, I made a point of very rarely visiting the school's loos. To be able to do this was indeed a blessing, no mean advantage. The technique – I think I can describe it as such – was to assume I wouldn't need them and consequently I didn't. Being free of that preoccupation made it so much easier to concentrate on lessons, and examinations, as well as to enjoy all there was to enjoy of school life. In fact I would go so far as to state that such freedom contributed in no small measure to my being, along with Rosemary and Margaret, consistently among the cream of the class.

Ah, those were the days, indeed. My Eden; my Paradise Lost. For that all changed, drastically, when at secondary school I developed a disorder that I've since realised must have been 'irritable bladder syndrome'. I've also since realised that it must have been a psychosomatic reaction to the severe trauma I underwent when I was compelled to leave 301, Granddad's home, and suddenly start a new and completely different life – along with a new school, a new role: that of stepdaughter in a new ménage. Including a brief intermediate phase staying with Daddy and his 'consort' – of whose existence, up till then, I'd had not the slightest inkling. At first she went out of her way to be nice to me – but, instinctively, I couldn't buy that. I realised she didn't like me – my first experience of that – and it showed in odd remarks she made.

There was also a new me to contend with, i.e. a different body, brought about by puberty. Plus of course the Blitz. I could have coped with those three challenges: puberty, Blitz, new school – after all, everyone else was coping with them – but the disintegration of my home, and my lifestyle, was another matter. The sudden and extreme change in my status was hard to take in my stride: I had to switch from being spoilt brat, apple of all the adults' eyes – to someone on the periphery. A leftover in fact, from a non-marriage – that of my parents. I had to try to fit into a very strange and previously undreamed of set-up: such was the household established by Mummy and my newly acquired stepfather – alias 'Step'. Although, fortunately, unlike Daddy's consort, he was not anti-me.

I must stress that he was a decent person and never in any way maltreated me. And as for my soon-to-be-acquired, strictly speaking, half-siblings – no one could love full siblings more than I did them, or they me. But for a while my nose was out of joint, I have to admit. It was the sheer change, its suddenness and my unpreparedness for it. It knocked me flat. I couldn't make sense of it. I couldn't cope. Something had to give – or, rather, protest. It happened to be my bladder. Its weapons: urgency and frequency of urination. This made my life misery – especially at school. Asking to be 'excused' – a request usually granted, but I could never be sure.

I needed help and couldn't get it. I tried. I went to doctors: one of them palmed me off with a placebo. 'Making a fuss about nothing' was another's diagnosis.

I was desperate for a cure, so I could get on with my life like other people – not just school work but ordinary living. Things like going to the cinema or the hairdresser were ordeals I strove to avoid, and as for coach trips – a school outing to St Albans with its wealth of Roman treasures was organised but I didn't dare go – much as I revelled in all things Roman.

I just had to get help! I took myself to hospital for tests – outpatient visits and then a stay inside for a fuller investigation under anaesthesia. After all that the findings were 'Nothing organically wrong'. Big deal! That meant 'No treatment available.' It seemed I would just have to live with this scourge – for that indeed was what it was.

At times it amounted to torment. It was hard enough to sit through forty-minute lessons, let alone three-hour-long exams. It was especially difficult when a request to be 'excused' had to be repeated when, quite soon after voiding, the wretched organ would fill up again and urgently need, again, to be emptied. Hoping to forestall this, I would avoid drinking – including the milk with my breakfast cereal or that served by prefects at the mid-morning break – I would pour this down the loo at my second, third or fourth visit.

Embarrassment was the worst part of all this. Some of my classmates made me a laughing stock, having to be 'excused' so often. This forced me to cook up an all-too-transparent ruse. 'Could I go and get my handkerchief?' How they saw through that! 'Who do you think you're kidding, Iris Briggs?'

My 'worst-case scenario' – wetting my pants there in front of them all – would be something I could never hope to live down – then, in my hypervulnerable days. Now, so many decades later, I'd take it in my stride. So what if I pissed in public? Hats off to Carol Thatcher who did just that, on TV!

But I have digressed, have I not, from the theme of Diana Garrod? Not all that much – because ever fresh in my mind is a scene in which one of her little charges, a boy called Eric, did indeed experience that worst-case scenario. The poor little chap lost control, and a tell-tale pool of urine appeared on his seat and the floor beneath. Far from reprimanding let alone ridiculing him Diana matter-of-factly wiped it up, with a reassuring, 'Not the end of the world!' And for good measure confiding, 'You know, this happened to me when I was at school.' She might have added, 'And look at me now.'

Yes. Just look.

"Queen and huntress,

Chaste and fair…"

All that and a whole lot more. She was simply one of the best people I have ever known.

Easter

Oh, I could write a sonnet
About your Easter bonnet...

Well, it didn't have to be a sonnet. Any sort of verse would do. When we were about eight, at the close of the spring term, two prizes were offered for the best poem – one from the boys, one from the girls. Appropriately enough, the prizes were in the form of Easter eggs.

The boys' was won by a certain Leonard Green. I hardly knew him; he was in my cohort, but not my class. The girls' was won by – guess who? Inspired by the Holiday Fellowship's community song book, where a ditty about the Red River Valley had long taken my fancy, my effort was based on that. I can just recall my last two lines:

And the tune of the Red River Valley
Will hum and sing you good night.

You could, I suppose, call it 'creative borrowing' à la Andrew Lloyd Webber. I have no recollection of what Leonard's poem was about.

We were triumphantly carrying our trophies home along the school path when Leonard tripped and dropped his – which at once shattered into smithereens. I felt so sorry for him! I don't suppose he'll ever forget that mishap – but perhaps he went on to win more lasting accolades. Did he go on writing? I wonder. Under a pseudonym, maybe; I haven't so far come across his real name anywhere in the literary columns. Kids of eight aren't drawn to attempt poetry unless there's some such urge lodged in their genes; it doesn't go away.

This incident made that particular Easter memorable – but they all were for one reason or another. Countless times Doris took me to St Albans – one of the best possible places you could be at Eastertide. The Cathedral is spectacularly dressed with spring flowers, especially the chapel of Queen Eleanor, mother of King Richard Coeur de Lion and King John – top goody and top baddy respectively – and John reputedly was her favourite! Amazing! Well, he does have Magna Carta to his credit…St Albans is one of several places where her cortège stopped on its way to her native Acquitaine; having died in England she was being carried home to be buried. Some of these stops are marked by a monument that has lasted till this day – Charing Cross is perhaps the most striking example.

I shall always be grateful to Doris for those many visits to St Albans; after London, the nearest city to Potters Bar, designated as such on account of its Cathedral. And that inspired me to write my first real poem, 'To the Virgin in St Albans Cathedral', at the age of twelve. No creative borrowing there – that was the real thing. It wasn't even juvenilia.

St Albans' other name is Verulam.* Rather than London, this was the capital of Roman Britain, taken over as such from the ancient Britons before them. It is very rich in remains from the classical past, including the only Roman theatre to be preserved in Britain. Museums, mosaics…My growing imagination thrilled to it all. Even to the paw-print of a dog in the two-thousand-year-old cement. It all nurtured the passion for everything Roman and Latin, indeed all things Caesarean, already burgeoning in me. I specify Caesarean because Verulam was the seat of Cassivellaunus the then leader of the Brits in its area; in 54 BC, on his second invasion of these islands, Caesar was intending to attack and take possession of it. But he had second thoughts more pressing matters, nearer home, (i.e. Rome), were requiring his attention and he therefore stopped short. Where, precisely? Maybe in the vicinity of Potters Bar! Maybe he actually set foot in what later became Mutton Lane! – it was probably a well-used artery even then. Well, he'd hardly be a more alien figure there than Herr von Ribbentrop. You can't rule it out.

Since the remit of this book is *people, places and incidents before, during and after WWII*, I reckon I can include Caesar and Cassivellaunus. They just make it into the 'before' category – albeit a long time before, somewhat longer than Charles Lamb or even Domesday Book, but no matter. They're in.

***

---

* Verulamium is the alternative spelling

Not only did I receive more Easter eggs one year than anyone else I knew (though doubtless the Little Princesses got more), excitedly I listened and watched as Granny came in through the kitchen door – bearing, I was sure, the best egg of all. I can still see her smile of pure joy. Now not only a grandmother but a great-grandmother myself, I know full well what it meant to her, getting for her best beloved the very best she could afford.

Nor did I go short on the 'Easter bonnet'. Everyone wore hats those days men, women and youngsters alike. Now comparatively few do; in fact the normal attire of fifty or sixty years ago is beginning to look like fancy dress. I've already mentioned my luxury frock from Daniel Neales which provoked the odd sneer from the 'common' kids on the council estate, 'Think you're posh, don't you!'

'Yes, I certainly do,' I sneered smugly back.

Ah! How I was spoilt then! That was a status quo not destined to last forever. Never mind.

'Tis better to be spoilt, then not,

Than never to be spoilt at all.

Napsbury

Taking the 313 green double-decker from Potters Bar, you bypass the Barnet Bypass and, going through South Mimms, strike the main road to St Albans. A few miles along this, in the vicinity of London Colney, you dismount and proceed some distance along a minor road which brings you to the gates of Napsbury. This is a word I don't enjoy writing. Or reading. Or hearing. It's the name of the mental hospital where my mother was incarcerated from 1930 to 1934, due to a post-puerperal condition caused by my birth. It was little understood then, not easily diagnosed. Consequently the right treatment was elusive – hardly surprising that, at first, she was pronounced incurable.

Hardly surprising, either, that I don't know the medical details – though, theoretically, they are ascertainable. Mummy herself told me her case was written up in a leading professional journal. I could have gone in search of this but, realising it would make distressing reading, shrank from doing so. It was sufficient for me that she was eventually released, despite that dire forecast, and able to resume life 'outside'.

Normal life? Not exactly. For her marriage had disintegrated. After a while, my father, doubly vulnerable as he had also lost his job in the Depression, had understandably found someone else. It would be uncharitable, and unreasonable, to blame him for that – and my mother didn't. She understood. She herself told me so. Generosity was one of the most striking aspects of her character and nothing illustrated it more than this.

But after she was discharged, cured despite that grim prognosis, could they not have come together again? 'For the sake of the children' – aka me? How I wish they had! However, that other person – 'there were three of us in that marriage' – wouldn't let go. That's the tragedy in a nutshell.

My grandfather it was who gave Mummy a home, alongside me, to come back to. I think the family's move to Potters Bar on his retirement must have been in order to be nearer Napsbury. Prior to that, for three years my grandparents together with my aunts and uncle, Mother's siblings, had been making every Sunday, the long and complicated journey from Wood Green – by train or Underground, then red double-decker followed by green, plus the walk from the main road to the Napsbury compound. And back. Relocation to Potters Bar more than halved that weekly lovingly made but exhausting trek. I don't know if I was ever taken along – I don't know if children were allowed to visit. I think if I had been taken I would have remembered (after all, I can recall a few things that happened when I was two or three) if only because it would have been dramatic or traumatic or both – earliest memories usually are.

So a new household came into being at 301 Mutton Lane and things went on swimmingly for some years. I was really happy. I never felt 'I haven't got a Daddy' because he never failed, peace and war alike, air raids or no air raids, to spend his Saturdays with me. Awaiting his arrival with intense eagerness I would watch from the window of our 'lounge' for the No. 29 bus to appear atop the crest of the London-side hill. Mummy and he would spend the time harmoniously enough together under Granddad's roof, along with other family members – Granny and Aunt Doris in residence, Elsie and Sid, with their spouses and offspring, often calling in. It was a perfectly content and seemingly normal household.

So why didn't they set up home together again? I don't know. But I do know they had loved each other to distraction throughout the four years of their engagement – to the extent of becoming the laughing stock of friends. And I believe he went on loving her even after he 'fell in love' with the other. 'Loving them both is breaking all the rules'. Some indication of this is that he kept many photographs of Mummy which, after her death, he gave to me and my children. (These must surely have been carefully hidden away from the consort throughout her entire tenure). As for her, possession is nine-tenths of the law, or, to vary the arithmetic, six days out of the seven prevail against the remaining one. For those six days, she had him all to herself but, come the seventh – reminiscent of a 'Sabbath' – she had perforce to yield him up to me. Unpleasant though she doubtless found this, she must have agreed to it even though it also meant his being at very close quarters with my mother. She knew how to play her cards; she knew, moreover, that this was a great chance to prove how 'broadminded' she was, how 'liberal'. Certain he'd reward her. Certain too that he loved her. I've asked myself time and time again – 'Why her?' Might as well ask, 'Why Camilla?' or 'Why Yoko Ono?' Or for that matter, 'Why Cleopatra?' Not that I put the 'consort' in that league – far, far from it – but the answer's the same, 'He loves her yeah, yeah, yeah.' A fact of life.

But back to Napsbury. Mummy told me quite a lot about it. About the doctors and nurses. Thank God, they treated their charges very humanely. In exemplary fashion I would say. Movingly, she spoke of the marvellous Christmases they gave them; incarcerated as she was, she experienced no fewer than four of these. They were sheer magic. She told me about the other patients too. Some of them were truly remarkable. In particular I was interested in a woman who claimed to be picking up radio signals. This was viewed as a symptom of mental disorder. But perhaps it was not? Perhaps she really was doing that, receiving messages from outer space. After all, are not learned societies devoting huge resources to finding any evidence of such communication? But she had not been taken seriously – instead, written off as a basket-case and kept indefinitely in the mental home. Then there was another patient who spoke fluent German without, she insisted, ever being exposed to it through everyday life or study. Could there be telepathic forces at work there? Again, research abounds in such areas but when a case like this appears, unsought, out of the blue as it were – how odd, how inappropriate that it is simply ignored, kept locked away in a place like Napsbury. But the inmate I found most fascinating was one Mrs Singh – married to an Indian who like my family visited unfailingly every week. I don't know anything about the medical side of her case, but her conversations with Mummy were extremely interesting. Focused as they were on the life of a British wife of a non-European, much of this information came in handy for me when I eventually found myself in such a situation. Among the facts that intrigued me particularly was the requirement to remove all bodily hair. 'Why don't English women do that anyway?' I asked Mummy, who replied, 'Some do, actresses for instance.' This begs a statistical survey!

Mother seemed to have got on so well with the people in the hospital, patients and staff alike – I wondered, didn't she miss them? They were, after all, a distinct community into which she'd fitted apparently easily. Didn't she ever want to go back and renew those contacts? Or did the reverse apply and she needed to distance herself as far as possible from 'all that'. After all, most prisoners on release from jail don't yearn to return and see the guards and old lags, no matter how friendly some of them might have been. In that sense she was like a person who'd lived some years on death row – in Mummy's case it wasn't the electric chair just along the corridor but such horrors as the strait jacket and the padded cell. She didn't talk about things like that – though she told me a great deal about Napsbury, some things were off limits, not be talked about – especially to the little kid I then was. Some aspects of mental hospitals are not the stuff of 'Listen with Mother'.

But I'd read about them, nonetheless, and wondered how close she'd come to the worst of them. Not least was stigma. Rampant in those days, it still hasn't completely gone away. As mentioned, London Colney was nearby and there was a phrase in current local usage – 'Colney Hatch', synonymous with 'loony bin'. Mother was of course aware of this and, I guess, hypersensitive about it.

Even without suffering the worst extremes such institutions may impose, it was surely enough for Mother to be, helplessly, on the receiving end of strict medical care for so long – and for much of that time with no end in sight. How natural if she'd yearned to get even, and be on the doling out end for a change. That must have been why, after her release, she developed such a keen interest in nursing, taking the relevant journals and lapping up every syllable of them. It was of course far too late for her to train and qualify as a doctor – though I've no doubt she would have been a good one. However, she did eventually become a nurse; under the auspices of the ARP and the war service everyone was required to do, she volunteered for nursing.

It was all part of compensation. She needed repayment for all she had lost – husband and home, and four years of her life – of her youth, moreover. And compensate she did in a big way. At first with several fun-geared years among that crowd of glamorous, charismatic friends. But that couldn't satisfy her for ever; it could only be stop-gap. She had to have a permanent, lasting compensation. This she was led to through her nursing, whereby she found her second serious partner, who was working as a stretcher bearer in the same project, who became my stepfather – 'Step'. With him she settled down at last to normality again. A happy normality, I truly believe, begetting my dearly loved brothers and sisters. Without, though, ever really forgetting Daddy. There again: 'Loving them both is breaking all the rules'.

Proof of that is, when the VIs and V2s were at their worst and Mummy, the children and I made our sole retreat from London to the beyond-range safety of Elsie's home in Lancashire, to see us off at Euston came both Daddy and Step – they could make no such escape since they had to stay in the capital for their work. They both kissed Mummy goodbye with heart and soul. And she them.

Mr Spink

Just between Hoskins the fishmonger and the Jewish confectioner Melsens there opened a brand new tobacconist. Its owner was Mr Spink. Being a kid I didn't have much occasion to purchase his wares. But I did a little – at Christmas, my every-year gift to Granddad was tobacco (Long John), since he loved to make his own cigarettes. And on Mummy's birthdays, I'd use the pocket money she herself had given me to get her favourite fags (Senior Service) plus some luxury chocolates.

Not being a regular customer, I didn't get to know Mr Spink very well. But I could see – it was as plain as a pikestaff – that he was a very good and decent person. Somehow such qualities generate a certain aura; you can't mistake them. So, along with everyone else in town I was aghast to learn one day that he had been diagnosed with a tumour on the brain. This was the first time I had heard there were such things and the horror of it wrought havoc with my imagination.

It would have wrought even more havoc had I known that, decades later, beloved Steve my brother would be stricken with the same scourge. Steve who, barely a month old, we (Mummy and I with Step) had rushed in the depths of the Blitz and the blackout from Southgate to Great Ormond Street children's hospital in central London. We couldn't easily use buses and Tube, so had to get a taxi – it wasn't easy finding one in the darkened bombarded streets. Although London taxis were not normally shared, air raids caused all rules to be broken and we were only too grateful when a fare already aboard allowed us to squeeze in with her – I can still recall that lady's face – the Lord only knows why she too was venturing forth, alone, in the wartime night – no one would do that unless they absolutely had to.

At Great Ormond Street Steve was (I have to call it miraculously) saved from a life-threatening condition – failure to suck. The wonderful staff there knew exactly what to do and he was put to rights in a matter of minutes.

Little could we have foreseen that what the great hospital preserved for him – life – would be wrenched away from him by the very same fiend that had attacked Mr Spink. God be praised that Mother and Step were not called upon to go through the anguish of a month-by-month hope-eroding ordeal – as, well before that happened, they themselves had 'passed on'.

No, I didn't buy lots of tobacco so I wasn't a regular. Probably I didn't make a lasting impression on Mr Spink. But he made a very lasting impression on me; in fact I was given a much stronger reason than a mere customer/vendor relationship to remember him for the rest of my life.

Dr Mary Allen

Dr Mary Allen was one of the undisputed top personalities of Potters Bar. Although she wasn't our GP – I mean the doctor on whose panel we were registered; that was Dr Porter – I was very well aware of her existence up there in the High Street, looking down as it were on her domain as it stretched from there northward, ever expanding, along with the town itself. Her reputation pervaded the whole community.

Once, when I was almost grown up, I went to her off my own bat, to see if she could shed any light on a disorder which had been plaguing me for quite a long time. It was basically a psychosomatic condition, little understood then – only years later was it labelled 'irritable bladder syndrome' – a companion-in-arms of 'irritable bowel syndrome' and equally capable of making someone's life misery. Both are known to be triggered by stress: I'd had plenty of that and needed someone I could discuss it with. Dr Mary Allen seemed to be that someone. She was the nearest I could get, then, to a psychiatrist and more effective than most of those I've later had recourse to, for this or that.

What made her so outstanding? Perhaps it was the hunch you had that you'd get from her more than a medical opinion, that what she'd give you would be more 'holistic'. It wasn't that female doctors per se were all that unusual those days – or female anything for that matter. In fact, throughout my entire growing up process I never once got the impression that women were inferior to men in any field whatsoever except sheer physical strength. A view backed up by all those 'charismatic' personalities we encountered personally – Mummy's glamorous entourage, and Doris's, Elsie's, and Sid's too – all the Rodwell siblings attracted friends of star quality. Not to mention the famous ones. The media of those days were crammed full with tales of doughty achievers who just happened to be female – singers, writers, actresses; presenters of worthwhile programmes on radio; politicians too, and pioneers, travellers and adventurers – such as Amy Johnson the aviator, Freya Stark the explorer – to name only some of the household names that continually sounded around us. None of them was considered in any way less than their male counterparts. There was something akin to these heroines in Dr Mary Allen. Her fame, albeit local, was like a flag flying high above her surgery, her colours nailed to the mast. You felt sure that, by visiting her, you'd come in contact with something first-rate you wouldn't forget in a hurry.

Once, at the secondary school, we were asked, in one of those delectable free periods given over to imaginative exercises. 'Who would you like to be if you were not yourself?' I'll leave aside the possible response, 'I don't particularly like being myself and wouldn't mind swapping with practically anyone.' The teacher who set this question was herself no mean role model. Not simply because of her main job, as sports mistress – in which she cut a dashing figure, always dressed in her on-duty 'uniform' – gym tunic with hemline well above the knee. She was pretty withal and had a great flair for filling those free periods with magic. In response to her question – 'Who would you like to be?' – I plumped for Dr Edith Summerskill, a prominent parliamentarian who was also a medical doctor. I don't know why I chose her – since I never hankered in the direction of either medicine or politics. But she was very renowned ('celebs' as such hadn't yet been invented; probably Zsa Zsa Gabor was the bellwether in that regard!). Whatever she said or did inevitably made news. And why should I have chosen a female anyway? I've never been particularly feminist. It seemed to me, at least in UK, that any woman who wholeheartedly wanted to accomplish anything could; provided she worked hard enough and single-mindedly, gender constituted no barrier. And while I was about it, I might just as well have 'voted' for Dr Mary Allen. Especially as she was someone I knew personally; she represented hope, and gender had indeed made a helpful difference in my case, as she was so much more approachable than a male doctor would have been regarding the kind of problem I had – involving as it did bladder and pudenda. I don't know how Dr Summerskill would have dealt with that; Dr Mary Allen did her best and it was pretty good.

It occurs to me: if asked that question now, what would my answer be? I think I'd decide it's unanswerable. There are, of course, one or two people I find it hard not to envy. Successful writers, for instance. But…You can't know what other people really are; it's just their façade that's facing you. What sort of baggage are they carrying? What sort of demons do they harbour, carefully hidden? That which makes them apparently so enviable may be counterbalanced by a whole lot of other stuff they'd rather be without, indiscernible to the observer.

Dr Mary Allen, as far as I could make out, had no such baggage and, judging solely by the amount of good she did, it would have been great being her.

A Matter of Course

To cross from one world to another, all you have to do is walk under the railway bridge that separates the Cranborne council estate from the Potters Bar Golf Course. 'The right side of the tracks' starts precisely there.

In the 1930s, as now, those who aspired to be admitted to the ranks of the posh saw golf as a reliable open sesame. Never mind out-tigering Tiger, or holing in one. You didn't even have to play golf. Just belonging to the club was enough.

Few in our family nursed such ambitions; on the whole we were 'content with our lot' with no urge to 'rise above our station'. Even if we didn't recognise it as such, being lower middle class suited us to a tee – we felt comfortable with it. But that didn't stop us enjoying long walks across the golf links of the affluent.

For us they represented a very good location for our marathon walks. Ours weren't in the Wordsworths' or even the Lambs' league but they were long walks all the same, usually undertaken on Sundays after lunch ('dinner' was the word used our side of the tracks). They served admirably to diminish the effects of the traditional roast meal, which simply had to include Yorkshire pudding and substantial "afters" (dessert). And they served too to keep intact our appetite for high tea – another Sabbath must.

Long walks were part of our life. It's odd, isn't it, that despite the much maligned British weather, most Brits incline towards the outdoor life. A bit of rain, or better still, drizzle, never puts them off; on the contrary, actually adding to their enjoyment. We were no exception.

So it chanced that one semi-fine or rather slightly drizzly Sunday afternoon, having navigated Darkes Lane and the leafy ways that form its tributaries, we found ourselves firmly striding out over the links in the direction of the Cranborne Bridge. From there it's only a few stones' throws back to 301.

More often than not, I went on long walks with Granddad, just the two of us, but this time we formed a fairish group, drawn from the combined Rodwell and Briggs clans. Including Daddy. Although it was Sunday, and Saturday was his time-honoured, never to be skipped Day for Me, he did make exceptions and additions – such as for a birthday or other special occasion. For instance, one Sunday evening he came to the Baptist Church service. Not 'to hear the parson shout', as in the non-nursery rhyme:

He goes to church on Sundays
To hear the parson shout.
He puts a penny in the plate
And takes a shilling out.

The Rev Aubrey Argyll D.D. was hardly the stereotype of a parson, and his distinguished sermons were definitely not examples of shouting. No. Most probably Daddy was there to discuss with him, and Mother, my proposed eventual baptism. Which, incidentally, never took place.

However that may be, that particular afternoon, having traversed Darkes Lane and the pleasant avenues that run into it – of which Miss Blunt's is the leafiest and prettiest – we boldly struck out on to the Golf Course.

These links were famous for a reason not connected with sport. Far from it. They were the reputed site of an unsolved crime – a murder to wit. About which rumour abounded; facts did not. Suspects didn't either – there was only one. but not a shred of evidence had so far been unearthed to support the belief, strongly held all over town, as to 'whodunit'. It wasn't a very comfortable feeling to rub shoulders with this guy in pubs or sit next to him on the bus – but there it was: not enough evidence to arrest, let alone convict. Mind you, capital punishment flourished in those days and there were many hoping to see this fellow 'swing'.

However, 'nothing we can do about it', far less allow such ruminations to spoil our walk. So we strode along with a will.

I'm amazed how I, a mite of four or so, managed to keep pace with the adults, but that's what I did. In fact, I actually 'outdid' them – Wordsworthian word, isn't it? – not in 'glee' but in sheer energy and stamina. Moreover I even used to boast, 'I'm never tired!' Couldn't understand what they meant if they said they were. Coals of fire! How those words have come back to taunt me in later years. Some decades into my life, for various reasons frequent fatigue became the norm for me; now I can't attempt even one tenth of the exertions so easily undertaken then, by me or my elders who, those days, were a good deal younger than I am now.

No matter! I was merrily gambolling along with them, sometimes holding hands, sometimes not, when suddenly I caught sight of a small round white object lurking in the rough. Gleefully I ran to 'fetch' it (much as Bob our terrier might – and he did sometimes accompany us on our outings) and presented it triumphantly to Mum and Dad, Granny and Granddad, with a proud. 'Look what I've found!' Expecting at the very least a pat on the back and delighted 'Clever girl!'

But! To my puzzled dismay, my kin's reaction was far from delight. Instead – what was it? Embarrassment? Annoyance, even? With me? As immediately there appeared out of nowhere an irate, disconcerted figure, exclaiming, 'What the…?'

What he no doubt meant was 'Why the hell can't you control that nuisance of yours?'

The nuisance itself was completely ignorant, feeling quite innocent of the 'crime' it had apparently committed. More than bewildered. Pondering, 'Whatever have I done wrong?' I thought I'd done something clever – like Bob got patted for. The injustice of it! It actually made me cry.

Daddy and everyone else were very upset then and strove to console me; 'Never mind, love! Don't take it to heart!' While doling out appropriate apologies to the intruder. And that, thankfully, was that. Hardly the time to expound to me the rules of the game.

Later, much later, years in fact – I reflected that our irate interrupter might have been a lot more disconcerted if, instead of a golf ball, he'd been presented with an eyeball. For such body parts were believed to be lying here and there, in some profusion, all over the Course. Since it wasn't a case of just one missing person, but several. And, as mentioned in another piece, this was not the only instance of a killer on the loose in our neck of the woods. In another case there was enough evidence to catch the culprit – he of the acid baths, from whom Maggie Roche had had such a narrow escape.

Whatever…However…That drizzly 1930s' Sunday afternoon we didn't let our thoughts dwell too long on such horrible subjects. We had other things to think about. Duly invigorated by exercise and big intakes of oxygen, we happily reverted to anticipating our upcoming high tea.

Arnhem Armada

My relocation to Southgate lasted four years. The reasons for it were twofold: (1) to be near my secondary school and (2) to form part of Mummy's new household with Step. I hated leaving Potters Bar but the move didn't cut me off from it. Even before I was given a bike, I would go frequently to 301 just to be with Granddad and Doris. It was always my first and foremost home – and always will be. Once BNAN 161, forever BNAN 161!

The trip of a few miles on the No. 29 bus, sitting on top at the front, was one of the happiest routines of my childhood and adolescence. But when the bike came on the scene a whole new fun element came with it. I remember when Mummy virtually ordered Step to go out and get it for me – like when she'd ordered him to go out and buy a wireless. In the latter case, I'd been crying because, at my new school, I was the only one in the class without one and consequently didn't know any of the pop tunes all the others were humming. 'Pistol packing Momma' was the one that hurt most – it was their favourite and I just didn't know it. I felt a real pariah! Moreover, one of my close friends – still just as close, sixty years later – was sharply critical. 'Don't have a wireless! It's inexcusable! Everyone has one these days!' Needless to say, that hurt even more. No one knew the reason for our deprivation and of course I didn't let on – we were very hard up; Mummy had even had to sell things, and so we just hadn't been able to afford a wireless. But Mummy had a way – a genius I'd call it, no less – for getting hard-to-get things. Especially when they were musts. My crying about the pop tunes had got to her. About the bike it was different: it wasn't a must; I didn't yearn for it, but simply felt it would be very nice to have one. And by that time too our finances had improved a little. So – Step went out and got it and boy, what a difference it made to my lifestyle! Here was another dimension: I'd graduated into another league, so to speak. Call it Serie A – or talk about 'upwardly mobile'.

I instantly put my brand-new Hercules to maximum use. I would think nothing of cycling to Potters Bar and back. Having arrived at 301, I would proudly tether my steed in the garden, by the trellis where the pink roses grew. Doris said, 'It's your treasure, isn't it?' Rejoicing as always in any treasure I had.

Rosemary too got a bike at exactly the same time. A case of keeping up with the Briggses – her mum could not have stomached for one second my having something Rosemary lacked. So she got her a Raleigh. We used to go riding together. I remember her waiting for me at our preferred rendezvous – the top of Stagg Hill. What a feat, getting up that steep gradient. Like a tour de force in the Tour de France. And what a compensation, going back, the sheer joy of free-wheeling the whole way down.

Funny how I enjoyed cycling, me who generally disliked sport – never forgetting to thank Marion who taught me. I was quite good at it too. I particularly enjoyed executing curves – most thrilling was zooming into Forestdale from Cannon Hill and, in the process, heeling over into a quasi-horizontal position – just like Valentino Rossi!

Funny too because, unlike Mummy, that *grande sportive*, here was one sport I enjoyed and she did not. I don't even know whether she could ride or not; at any rate, I never saw her on a bike. As for Daddy, I tried to teach him, but gave up! I'm no Marion!

But I digress. Some trips to Potters Bar were without benefit of bikes and harked back to the days of my long walks with Granddad, the "I never feel tired" days of my early childhood. So it chanced that, one fine summer afternoon in 1944, he and I, together with Doris, set out from 301 to South Mimms, always a favourite destination of ours. From there we could see North Mimms, about a mile off. We never went there. In fact there was practically nothing to go there for. It's not even a hamlet, let alone a village, just a scattering of odd buildings. Warrengate Farm was one of them; another was a biggish house, a minor stately home, granted 'for the duration' (of the war) to Queen Wilhelmina of the Netherlands, a royal refugee from Nazi occupation.

By contrast, South Mimms has been for centuries a proper village, a distinct community, complete with its church – St Giles. The vicar's daughter, Miss Gower, was my very first teacher at Cranborne Infants. Moreover, since it marks the end of the 29 bus route, which starts in Victoria and weaves through Westminster and the West End, 'South Mimms' emblazoned on its brow, the cosmopolitan denizens of Piccadilly and Leicester Square are well aware of its existence.

It's a nice place to live in, too. It boasts some very pretty gardens. And there are several significant buildings – notably Clare Hall, for many years a medical centre: it played a big role in fostering the ARP's health-related activities that brought Mother and Step together – she a nurse, he a stretcher-bearer. And it's very interesting to me that WHO eventually set up a Centre of Excellence in South Mimms – one of the very few in UK and I think quite a coincidence in view of my decades-long career with WHO in Egypt.

That sunny Sunday afternoon in 1944 we were taking our ease on a seat by St. Giles when we suddenly noticed the sky was full of planes. Packed full of them. A veritable armada was passing overhead. Whatever could this be? Unheard of at this time of day – though big fleets often flew over at night, our squadrons setting out to bomb Germany – but even then, in nothing like these numbers. Whatever was in the air? Literally and figuratively. Puzzled, we gazed and gazed. They kept on coming. And kept on going, relentlessly, towards the south-east.

We didn't know it then, when it was actually happening, but this was a planned strike into Europe, a precursor of D-Day. Intended to land at Arnhem, in Wilhelmina's Holland. A doomed precursor – it didn't succeed. The Nazis' intelligence had heard about it and they were waiting for them. Many lives were lost.

Shortly afterwards I wrote about it – unashamed juvenilia this time. One verse went like this:

O'er English fields we saw them glide
Who rode into the jaws of hell
And as they went, the countryside
Seemed strangely smiling in farewell.

Juvenilia, yes, but it couldn't have been more heartfelt. I was so proud to have seen what we saw. Part of our 'finest hour' – people like Pat Garland and his brothers were up there, prepared to give their all – their lives, their futures – for us. And for so many of them, that was exactly what they gave.

In pace requiescant.

The King's Stammer

When the just abdicated King Edward-VIII declared, 'God Save the King!' it sent shivers down our spines. Fifty million of us were clamped to the wireless – apart from the sheer drama, we were so thrilled and delighted that someone we liked and admired so much, someone we were so truly fond of, was going to be the head of our family. What a fine outcome to a crisis that had seemed well-nigh insoluble. The Mrs Simpson crisis.

But there was one person listening to that most famous of all broadcasts who was not thrilled or delighted. Quite the reverse. And that was the new King himself. For him, this development meant he must face a future filled to the brim with pain and struggle. Every day fraught with challenges requiring him to muster all his strength. Yet – he accepted it, utterly determined to do, come what may, what he saw as his duty. All the obligations that would now devolve upon him – most would entail the thing he dreaded most: speaking in public. Dreaded because of the speech impediment that had plagued him all his life. But he had no choice. Duty – that was the keystone of his character. Perform it he must. And he did. Day after day, year after year, the whole nation agonising with him as he fought, in speech after speech, to get out word after word. Every one of his 'subjects' felt for him, quite irrespective of political alignment. Or anything else. How we felt for him! Here was a human being, who just happened to be royal (that was neither here nor there) with whom we could all empathise, coping with a handicap anyone would find daunting – 'There but for the grace of God go I.' Yes, we agonised and even writhed as he battled to get those syllables out.

'Just doing my job,' he would no doubt have said, like heroes do when asked by the media, 'However did you do it?' His job. He never shirked it. He went on doing it till the last day of his life.

How right King Edward had been in extolling the partner his brother had been blessed with. Such a partner as he himself had so far been denied. One who would help and support her beloved 'Bertie' every step of the way. His triumph over disability was her triumph too. Those of us who witnessed all that can never possibly forget.

What an exemplary pair they made. You don't have to be a monarchist to appreciate that. Even communists would surely concede, those two were the best possible mother and father this nation could have had in that dark hour of need – as providentially sent as Churchill. Our darkest and indeed our finest hour, when we were confronting Hitler. It was proposed at one stage that King George-VI be given the title 'George the Good'; not a soul, surely, would fail to concur with that idea.

With one exception. Once upon a time I knew a person (who shall be nameless) who not only failed to writhe and agonise with George the Good but actually ridiculed him, making cruel fun of the defect he strove so valiantly to conquer. Never again did I encounter such an aberration from the norm and I ardently trust I'll never do so. Anyone capable of such insensitivity has to be beyond the pale. Instinct warns us to give such persons ('hopefully' there aren't too many of them) an exceedingly wide berth. One feels there's nothing they wouldn't stoop to, if they're base enough to mock the King's stammer.

Singing in the Shelters

We had big playing fields at both schools. But come the war, the Cranborne ones were largely dug up to make room for air raid shelters. While the Southgate County ones were not. Funny that, since Southgate is in Greater London and Potters Bar isn't; the assumption must have been that the former would be more at risk than the latter. But this proved not to be the case: Potters Bar received more hits and suffered more casualties than Southgate.

As mentioned, air raids – either the RAF's or the Luftwaffe's – didn't usually take place during the day/school hours. But just in case – the shelters were there. And we did have occasion to use them quite a lot since, whether planes came over or not, from time to time the air-raid sirens wailed.

We had to face the possibility of being stuck underground for hours – perhaps even days. Fortunately that never happened; the longest we were confined didn't amount to more than about an hour at the most. But we had to be prepared; hence each one of us brought to school every day a supply of 'iron rations' (in which chocolate figured prominently). Together with our gas-masks and of course our school work; all this had to be lugged to school and back every day for six years, i.e. 1939–1945.

The shelters were quite large – hardly paragons of comfort; 'utilitarian' is the best word to describe them. They consisted of cylinders, such as are used in sewerage systems. An adult could barely stand upright in them while each was long enough to accommodate a class of approximately thirty children seated half on each side, a teacher in charge, with a toilet at each end.

It was a test of ingenuity on the part of the teachers to help their pupils pass the time. To a certain extent it was 'lessons as usual' but there had to be some relief. Some sort of entertainment was called for. And who would provide it? We ourselves of course – who else? The plethora of entertaining devices that amuse people today just didn't exist then.

So – singing came into its own. We soon got though the songs we'd had dinned into us in music classes. Stuff like 'The Vicar of Bray', 'Here's to the Maiden of Bashful Fifteen', 'What Shall we do with a Drunken Sailor?' odd that one very rarely hears these except at school, yet even so everyone knows them. You can't escape them. We soon got to the end of all those. So, what next? What else but the pop tunes of the day? – those churned out regularly by the likes of Geraldo and Henry Hall, as well as the hits of Bing Crosby and the Andrews Sisters. These could hardly be sung in chorus by the whole class; they called for solo renditions. None of my confrères felt equal to that – but I had no such qualms! I knew I could do it! Secretly I felt I was competent/capable as Dorothy Carless or Brian Lawrence, so I confidently launched, solo, into such numbers as 'Deep Purple', 'South of the Border', 'Hang out the washing on the Siegfried Line'. Turning to Bing's repertoire (I must stress all this predated Sinatra by several years) and Bing was undisputed king of crooners (and still is, for my money): 'Beautiful Dreamer' and 'Moonlight Becomes You'. As for the Andrews Sisters, 'Pennsylvania Six Five Thousand' was my ditty of choice. I loved to give it all I'd got. I drew the line at 'An Apple for the Teacher' – too sensitive, with Mr Bath sitting right there at the end of the cylinder.

Thus, I acquired a real taste for 'crooning'. And, dare I say it, some expertise. I felt I had the audience eating out of my hand. I even had 'fans' with their 'requests' and as far as I could I complied. I got a tiny glimpse of what it's like to be a celeb.

But – and this is a very big but – I could only do all this because there in the shelters we were in darkness. No one could see my flaming face or the twitching nerve in my cheek that were sure to manifest once the limelight was on me. Giving rise to real stage fright and simply stopping me from getting up in a theatre and performing. It hadn't always been like that – as a four and five-year-old I'd been quite untroubled by those drawbacks. I just don't know what rendered me a year or so later so prone to them. And there in the shelters, simply because there was no one to see them, my face didn't blaze, my nerve didn't twitch. And the same applied, years later when, childhood behind me and adolescence in full swing, I would sing solo in the chapel of a Kensington convent. Hidden at the back, in the choir (I was the only non-nun among them) alongside the little organ so masterfully played by Mother St. Charles, hidden – I could let rip and again, give the music all I'd got. This time, it was Spanish and Latin hymns and carols; one Easter we did a whole Mass. And again for an appreciative public – people came to the convent from all over London to hear us give voice to an otherwise largely unknown repertoire. Yes, the audience enjoyed it and so did I.

In like spirit I relished and looked forward to those crooning sessions in the shelters. They almost (but not quite) counterbalanced the dread of hearing the air-raid warning. But even they couldn't diminish the relief of hearing the all clear – surely one of the most blessed sounds ever heard.

Sleeping in the Shelters

Although Mr Magnus cut a gap in the fence between our two backyards, intending to give us access to the Anderson shelter in their garden, we never actually used it for that purpose. We hesitated to inflict ourselves on the Magnuses; the space in the Anderson would hardly accommodate two five-member families. Nonetheless, that gap served another, equally laudable aim; to remind us, for ever, of the real neighbourly concern – indeed, love – existing between the two households. Never have I seen put into practice so strikingly the holy precept, 'Love thy neighbour as thyself'.

As for 'love thy grandchild…' Although we at 301 made do with our shelterless home throughout the raids, there were some places in it, as in every house, deemed safer than others. The grown-ups unanimously gave the safest one, that under the stairs, to me, 'the little'un'. Granddad, Doris and Mother all continued to sleep in their vulnerable bedrooms. (Granny had passed on in April 1940 before the Blitz started in earnest). I didn't appreciate their self-sacrifice then. Now, it's another matter. I can't help feeling guilty that I never thanked them – not only for that but for all the care and concern they lavished on me, since taking me on a few months old, when Mother was hospitalised*. After her release on my fourth birthday Mother assumed her share of responsibility for me but all the others continued to provide a very great deal. My welfare, my health, my safety always at the top of their priority list. Shelter from air raids was only one aspect.

As mentioned elsewhere, in 1941 I had to leave Potters Bar. The reasons were twofold. Intertwined. Firstly, I had to move on from elementary Cranborne to a secondary school; the one chosen for me, mainly because my father had also

---

* I should put on record that for a short while immediately following Mother's incarceration, I was cared for by Muriel Craig, wife of paternal Uncle Arthur. Then Granny took over.

attended it, was situated some miles away in Southgate. Secondly, Mother was about to set up her new home with Step. After much house hunting on which I accompanied them, they chose a beautiful place in Forestdale, in walking distance of the school. It made sense, I suppose, that I should form part of the new place with my mother, but I hated leaving 301 and would happily have commuted to and from school like my neighbour Audrey Smith, on the No. 29 bus. Perhaps – no mean bonus – sharing a seat with Derek Stockbridge!

But the Forestdale home was indeed delightful. I can see now that it was more 'upmarket' – there was no such word those days – than Mutton Lane, full of professional people – chartered accountants, solicitors and the like. (Hardcore middle class plus a sprinkling of upper). But let markets get stuffed! 'There's no place like home/be it ever so humble' – never were truer words sung.

At first, for me, Forestdale was more of a novelty than a home. But that changed when Steve was born there – the first of my four siblings. For the record again: I was alone with Ma when he was born. Alone that is except for Natushka. We two were the first, after Mother herself, to welcome Steve into the world. When labour pains started I rushed to the neighbours to get a doctor. I was only eleven – and a very naïve eleven at that – didn't know anything about labour or indeed that Ma was pregnant. She was in severe pain and I was scared stiff. It was a Sunday morning and we had only moved in five days before, didn't know a soul in the district.

I'd been an only child till then – spoilt-brat into the bargain, focus of everyone's attention. At first, again, I was jealous. No question about it, my nose was out of joint. But that changed too – very soon, when, only weeks old, Steve was critically ill and we had to rush with him – by night in the middle of the Blitz and the blackout – to Great Ormond Street hospital – where he was, you can only call it miraculously, saved. From that moment on he became my number one love. So, since love is what gives a house meaning, within quite a short time I was feeling at home in Southgate as well as in Potters Bar.

Ours was rented premises, which we could just afford by the skin of our teeth. But it might have been designed with me in mind. For one thing it was chock full of books – Children's Encyclopaedia, Jane Eyre, the Russian short-story writers – it was here that I made the acquaintance of all of those, devouring them avidly. Plus, I'm sorry to confess, liberally scribbling my own comments in them. Heaven alone knows what the owners of No 28 thought when our tenancy came to an end and they got all their stuff back. Some pretty puerile/juvenile ideas were among those marginal notes of mine! The bookcases also boasted several anthologies, many more classics and plenty of relatively unknown works. Lots of poetry. I couldn't have asked for more.

This second home of mine had several other charming features, some of them novelties for me. Notably a garage (a car in it, but not used – anyway, none of us could drive and, this being wartime petrol was severely rationed). There was too a greenhouse where Step, Steve in his arms (and sometimes in mine) would potter about; a frog had taken up residence there; we dubbed him "wog-wog". The garden was richly planted throughout – not up to Granddad's standards, but getting on that way. Most delightful of all for me, when we moved there in November, was an abundance of crysanthemums. 'Chrysanthemum throne' indeed – I don't know if Mr Fujihito (whom we had yet to meet, living just down the road) also had these flowers in his garden but I reckon he jolly well ought to have had.

Among No 28's many assets was its own custom-built shelter in the garden. Posher than Andersons or Morrisons, but posh is as posh does – a shelter's sole raison d'être being to save life. Like that of the people next door, it lay half in their territory and half in ours. Theirs was an above – ground structure but ours, like the Andersons, partly below. Theirs was rectangular, ours spherical, somewhat igloo-shaped, covered in summer with a blue wealth of cornflowers. Inside, you had to go down a few steps into a sort of ante-chamber and thence into the refuge proper. That was quite small. It was all concrete; by rights it should have been damp and dank, but I don't recall ever feeling cold there, much less catching cold. Perhaps because of the wartime rations so carefully allotted to give us all optimum health protection. And perhaps because the design of the shelter was so well thought through and executed. We kept a stock of necessities there, including iron rations like at school. And it was serendipitous that there was an outdoor loo a few steps away by the kitchen door. We made ourselves as comfortable as we could. Not even deprived entirely of entertainment – I used to embellish the concrete walls with doodles and scribblings such as quotes from Caesar's Gallic Wars which we were doing then at school – he was already my favourite historical personage.

Our Blitz routine would start before bedtime when, whatever the weather, we would sally forth through the garden carrying all our essential gear, shelter-bound. The symphony of the night was about to begin – its overture being the air-raid warning with its unforgettable, dreaded melody.

Soon after, the Luftwaffe would be heard approaching, a bomb exploding now and then, near or far, the anti-aircraft arsenal hitting back fortissimo. Searchlights arched across the sky.

Sometimes for months on end we would follow this regimen. But the Blitz varied in its intensity – in London and elsewhere too. Other cities were often specially targeted, cultural centres chosen purposely at times – part of the attack on our national morale – the so-called Baedeker raids, so named after a well-known tourist guide book. Thus it was that Exeter, Coventry, York, among many others, got their own special Blitz night when they were pounded mercilessly non-stop. But from time to time, there was a let-up, a lull, possibly lasting months, and we would allow ourselves to sleep in our beds. No luxury was ever longed for more passionately than that! Throughout the difficult, shelter-confined periods, we would dream of sleeping in our blessed bedrooms – dream as of a veritable paradise lost.

Our refuge area had space enough for two bunks, one up and one down. Mummy had the top one with my brothers – Steve, a toddler by now and Tony the new baby whom she was breastfeeding. While I had perforce to share the lower one with Step. I didn't feel comfortable about that, though I must emphasise very strongly that he always behaved in exemplary fashion, never making the slightest inappropriate move or gesture. Moreover, to make things even more correct, we slept in head-to-toe position (like a Pisces sign) so as far as possible we weren't actually 'sleeping together'. (After all, we had little choice – other than to remain night-long in our bedrooms and risk the effects of bombing, such as blast and shrapnel, not to mention the whole house collapsing on top of us. The only danger we risked here was a direct hit).

Nonetheless, I couldn't relax. I couldn't help feeling uneasy as I went down those steps every night. I would offer up a prayer as I did so, worried lest, in spite of all precautions, something untoward might happen. This anxiety couldn't have done me much good and I think it affected my school work. The last year of the Blitz (with the added menace of the V1s and V2s) coincided with our crucial (fifth form) 'matric' year – the name used then for the school-leaving exam, or GCSE as it was later called. Pupils needed to be in good mental shape to do themselves justice and I'm afraid I fell short of that a little. Everyone had to cope with the stresses of the war – the raids and the associated fears and pressures – but I was the only kid in class having to deal with such a peculiar situation at home. A year or so earlier I had done spectacularly well (like at Cranborne), coming top of the class three terms running, but I began to lose ground, some classmates overtook me and that matric year I came only fifth. Still – I passed. Not with *magna cum laude* like one of my friends but with 'distinction'. Fair enough.

As we emerged from the shelters in the morning, the bombing having stopped, the Luftwaffe (or that part of it not shot down) having gone home 'on a wing and a prayer' – like our RAF/Garland heroes returning from similar sorties over Germany, we'd look around to ascertain, as far as we could, what had happened during the night. Had any neighbouring house been hit? No doubt, as the morning wore on, we'd hear more – had anyone nearby been hurt? Or killed? Anyone we knew? We couldn't expect to get such details on the wireless. They couldn't give results of every single raid: there were far too many of them. Alvar Liddell and Bruce Belfrage – the star anchors of those days – had more global things to tell us about.

One local happening, however, did make the headlines. That was the Bounds Green Underground disaster. Like at most London Tube stations, Bounds Green – the next-but-one to us on the Piccadilly Line (Arnos Grove was the nearest) was full of shelterers. Hundreds of people repaired there each night, sleeping on bunks on the platforms. Many had done this year after year. And made of this place a veritable home from home – having developed the know-how for minimal comfort, achieving a modus vivendi packed with camaraderie. On the whole it was an excellent arrangement, any inconvenience outweighed by many benefits. It was like that too in scores of other stations throughout the Tube network; truly 'underground', these places might have been designed with air-raids in mind. Their safety record was phenomenal. One night, however, Bounds Green became the exception. A direct hit.

In pace requiescant.

Card-carrying Colonists

Once upon a time there was a lot more to a packet of cigarettes than just the fags. There was an all-important adjunct, namely a card – as *de rigueur* then as a health warning is today. Each card was one in a series (of thirty if my memory serves me right) on a particular theme; each focused on a personality prominent in that area, with a portrait on one side and on the other a brief biographical sketch. The aim of card-holders was to acquire a complete series.

One got addicted. Kids pestered their elders – maybe some actually bought cigarettes with their pocket money just to get the card.

I wasn't exactly a champion of this pastime but I did manage to acquire two complete sets. And how I cherished them! One was about cricket and its leading figures; the other about dignitaries taking part in the Coronation – it was 1937 – clad in their full traditional regalia.

From this it may be deduced that, in UK at any rate, the whole exercise was Brit-geared – Coronation and cricket. How Brit can you get?

Though I took much pride in my two collections at the time, nowadays I can barely recall any of the individuals featured in them. Exceptions are the Viceroy of India and, more especially, the Vicereine: Lady Edwina Mountbatten – they don't come more aristocratic than that. I recall that she was buried at sea with full naval honours. The Mountbatten family was not just *plus royaliste* but *plus royal que le roi* – as no doubt Prince Charles himself would be the first to confirm. He lost his beloved and distinguished uncle, Lord Louis, to IRA terrorists (who also mowed down others including the Mountbatten grandson aged fourteen). As Charles reminded people at a memorial service for victims of another outrage, 'I know what it means to lose dear ones to terrorists; I know how it feels.'

Regarding the cricket series, it highlighted some superstar players – among them, of course, Australians and even one or two Indians (such as Ranjit Singh). Those nations, then as now, could give England more than a good run (or runs!)

for her money. Don Bradman, Walter Hammond and Denis Compton were the most obvious heroes but my preference went to a non-household-name performer, namely one Hardcastle, who played for Nottingham. For the uninitiated – that is, the even more uninitiated than I for I'm no cricket aficionado – it may be noted that in England cricket is based on counties. As for Nottingham itself, surely no one but a Brit would give a Friar Tuck about that city's team. Or, for that matter about the Coronation retinue, clad in their full ceremonial garb: to modern-day eyes this looks remarkably like fancy dress.

Indeed, those cards per se seem pretty archaic now. Obsolescent to say the least. Reflecting another day, another age. An age when Britannia did indeed rule the waves and we all thought that right and proper. When half the world was coloured pink to denote the British Empire – likewise, that was OK by us. We kids accepted all that as the norm – we were little colonists in the making and the cigarette cards reinforced this attitude.

They were part and parcel of our childhood and our growing up process, taking us up to WWII and beyond. Part and parcel of the then environment. Like the roses in our summer gardens and the snow in our winter ones. They were a fetish maybe, and they faded out – cigarettes themselves likely to follow suit? – other fetishes taking their place: computers, mobile phones, hols on the Costa Brava – you name it. But the snow and the roses and the gardens remain.

Likewise the Empire has gone, and along with it so much of the pomp and circumstance it engendered. But England's still there. And so is cricket! Not to mention the royals!

Plus ça change……

How not to Earn Five Bob

At Cranborne we'd been constantly urged to engage in nature study, doing things off our own bat, like going out looking for newts and tadpoles. I didn't mind doing this in moderation; it didn't seem too difficult. The countryside was still on our doorstep – we had encroached upon it, so to speak, stepping up the urbanisation process, when we settled in Potters Bar in 1933. In front of our house then were open fields – as they probably had been uninterruptedly since the days of the Domesday Book.

There were still plenty of places for tadpole and newt hunts. Notably at the end of Bridgefoot where there's a sizeable stream; it goes on to run under Cecil Road, the last leg of the A111 before it comes to an end at South Mimms. So you can choose between two routes for your nature study spree – either along the main road, by bus if you like, or, the rambler's choice, walking the whole length of Bridgefoot till you come to that specimen-rich stream.

Marion and I had opted for the latter when we set out one fine summer's day, intent on grabbing a haul to impress Miss Garrod or Mr Bath or both (we weren't in the same cohort, Marion being one year younger than me).

Accordingly we tramped to the end of Dugdale, where it forks – to the left going along Sawyer's Lane towards Bentley Heath – one of my favourite long-walk destinations with Granddad – which in turn takes you for a short stretch outside the confines of Potters Bar, bringing you on to the Great North Road (aka the A1000), not far from the site of the Battle of Barnet. There it was that, in 1475, Warwick the Kingmaker 'met his Waterloo' and, nearby, the Martians landed in HG Wells's 'War of the Worlds'. To the right of the fork lies Bridgefoot – not so much a country lane as a ramshackle way through woods. An isolated way to say the least. You could be forgiven for thinking Piccadilly Circus and Leicester Square were light years distant, instead of a mere hour's ride from South Mimms on the 29 bus.

Looking back with hindsight, Bridgefoot seems to me more than a little scary. Children, the elderly, or indeed anyone short of a super-armed Superman, would be extremely ill-advised to go wandering through it alone. Yet Marion and I, in our innocence and ignorance, were about to do just that when we caught sight of a figure in the field facing us at the end of Dugdale. A young chap was waving and beckoning, with a cordial. 'Hello, there!' We were curious, so we returned his greeting equally cordially, 'Hello!' What had he got to tell us? What did he want? Information, maybe: e.g. which way to Bentley Heath? It wasn't immediately apparent. But surprisingly he went on: 'Would you like to earn five bob?' (Five bob is colloquial for five shillings.)

We looked at each other, puzzled. Earn five bob? Well, why not? There were plenty of things we could spend it on – for instance a few bars instead of just one of our beloved Fry's Chocolate Sandwich, or treating ourselves to the luxury version of Walls Ice Cream peddled by the 'Stop Me and Buy One' man, who cycled around town with a cartful of such goodies – we'd get some super-wafers filled to overflowing rather than the cheaper cornets we usually bought.

We considered the offer.

'Maybe,' we answered cautiously. 'But – what would we have to do?'

The answer was monosyllabic – a monosyllable moreover that we had never heard before; we hadn't a clue what it meant. Simply, 'Fxxk.'

Although we didn't understand, we sensed this was something dangerous. Something we had to get away from prontissimo. So we did just that – turning back into Dugdale and running as fast as our little legs could carry us. Would he follow and attack us? We daren't stop to look around. Our fear was that he'd try to kill us. Like everyone else in town, we knew about the murders on the Golf Course and elsewhere. It didn't occur to us that there might be another form of attack – we just didn't know about that. We simply ran and ran and ran. Fortunately there was a hedge between him and the road it would slow him down a bit, giving us something of a head start. We knew we had to get fast to a built up area. By the fork there weren't any buildings, such as houses, shops, or offices. Nor did we meet anyone on the road who might help us if attacked – or at least be a deterrent witness.

We ran till we were breathless. When at last a house or two appeared we felt it was safe to stop and look around. Were we being followed? No, thank the Lord. No sign of the 'chap'. So we calmed down, got our breath back and proceeded on our way home at a normal pace. Calmed down superficially, that is. Inside, we were still churned up and remained so for quite a time to come.

Neither Marion nor I got to know the meaning of that word till quite a good while afterwards. But somehow we'd sensed all along that it had to do with a taboo and was therefore unmentionable to our families. At any rate, neither of us dared to tell them about this incident till much later.

Looking back, so many years on, I can't help reflecting how right Rosemary's mother had been to chaperone her everywhere she went, till she was old enough to think for herself and be properly aware of dangers. I also reflected how one of my classmates, June Pratt, lived near the scene of that frightening encounter, in a farm just along Sawyer's Lane. She would have to pass by the fork twice every day, going to and from school. Who knows who might be lurking there, or in the murky depths of Bridgefoot, waiting to pounce on the unwary – child or adult. But the menace of course could be anywhere, anywhere at all where the defenceless might find themselves face-to-face with some predator. Rapist or killer or mere molester.

In those days, you didn't hear much, if anything, about child abuse, on the wireless or in the press. Staple fare of the media today. Let alone 'porn' hard or soft, the term hadn't yet been coined. But then, the media itself was far from developed – no TV, no Internet. Word of mouth was a bit more explicit; you sometimes heard vague references to people being 'interfered with' – a euphemism triggering curiosity, for there again I hadn't a clue what it meant.

Eventually one finds out. One lives and learns – a lot more than the stuff taught in schools. It can be a slow process; it can depend an awful lot on luck. Food for thought here. Shouldn't the realities of practical living – unpalatable though some doubtless are – be high up on the teaching agenda? If things like trigonometry and algebra are – why not the 'facts of life'? After all, they are an intrinsic part of 'nature study'.

As for newt and tadpole hunting – it simply isn't worth it. We could learn all that from books. As for venturing down Bridgefoot – let ramblers do that, if they must, but en masse. Safety in numbers. As for the rest of us – even any budding Darwins or Huxleys – teachers or parents or other responsible grown-ups should be around to hold their hands. Otherwise – to hell with do it yourself! For that matter, to hell with newts and tadpoles.

Primrose

A primrose is a delicate flower, and Primrose was a delicate girl.

Coming down Mutton Lane from Bridge House, John Morris's homestead, you quite soon pass on your left a biggish house with a biggish drive-in (though in those wartime days no one actually did drive in – no car, no petrol). This being an old house, more likely it was designed for horse and carriage. I guess it has been there much longer than Bridge House or perhaps even than the bridge itself, spanning as it does the railway – a comparatively recent addition to the Mutton Lane scene. The big old house has certainly been there much longer than the facing row of buildings, erected post WWI; it might even have been there when Charles and Mary Lamb ventured into Potters Bar in the early nineteenth century. I reckon it was originally a farmhouse but, as urbanisation proceeded, the farm ceased to exist as such, reverting to fields which were later built on.

Whatever…this house was the home of one of my classmates, Primrose Roberts. I remember her well. If anyone was ever 'conspicuous by her absence', it was she. In fact that phrase might have been coined with her in mind, she was so often labelled 'absent' at the daily roll-call; we each had to answer to our name with a hearty affirmation, 'Present!' This Primrose rarely did. I don't even recall seeing her in class, or exactly where she sat; I can place almost all the others. Nor does she feature in any of the annual class photographs. Why was she so out of the picture?

The reason was her health. The primrose is a fragile flower and Primrose was a fragile child. It wasn't easy for her to get to school – in those days there weren't any others nearby of Cranborne's calibre. Not for Primrose cycling to school like John – in fact he was the only one of my classmates who did so. And to walk would have been too strenuous for her. No Roger Limbrey she – she'd have been exhausted well before arriving in class. So she probably took the bus – two or three stops along. But in those days too, cheap though transport was compared with today, it could have been an item to reckon with in a family's budget.

Delicate and fragile. Barely equal to life's struggle – that was Primrose. How different from her famous namesake, Margaret Hilda Roberts. Someone all too conspicuous by her presence – be it at school, or you-know-where: parliament and the halls of fame. Margaret Hilda née Roberts, that is, her maiden name overshadowed by that other, derived from her husband, that she propelled to international celebrity and embellished with a title: Baroness Thatcher. A far cry indeed from our little Primrose.

Never mind. Perhaps our schoolmate after all went on to lead an enjoyable and richly fulfilling life as that of any Iron Lady. I hope so. I hope especially that her health improved – as it might well have. So many advances in medicine have taken place since our Cranborne days. Health is the key to so much. But not everything. You can be happy – albeit by the skin of your teeth – without too much of it. Like money. Life has many things to offer, and getting to school easily and always answering 'Present!' aren't the only ones.

Pivotal Point

Now what exactly is the pivotal point? I'll tell you. It's the very centre of Potters Bar – as you can see from the map – where the east-west, north-south lines bisect each other. The very heart of the place. And appropriately enough it's in Mutton Lane, the town's main street (another fact which the map clearly shows) aka the A111. We at 301 were only a few yards from that pivotal point. For me, it was the scene of several memorable events – centre-stage, as it were.

For starters, it was where I met Granny when I returned, ignominiously, from my first visit, aged five, to the dentist. I could already see her expression from some way off; I knew she was eagerly looking forward to hearing how I had acquitted myself at that, my first encounter with 'surgery'. I felt no shame in telling her I hadn't acquitted myself at all. Mission far from accomplished. In fact, I'd made myself quite unhandleable, all but kicking the dentist in the stomach. An occupational hazard as, many years later, my son, who happens to be a professor of paediatric dentistry, confirms. He advises students how to tackle such difficult child patients and how to protect themselves optimally against such onslaughts.

It has been said, by no less an authority than Agatha Christie, that there are few places where one is more vulnerable than in the dentist's chair. With respect, I beg to dispute that. You may think that the man wielding the drill has the upper hand but it ain't necessarily so, when a naughty spoilt kid of five has the upper foot. Anyway, that day in 1935, after valiant attempts to deal with recalcitrant me, they'd been forced to give up and send me home untreated.

As an infant I'd been nicknamed 'Timmy' – 'the Timid' might well have been added. A fitting title, as I was indeed a tiny little coward. But, thank the Lord, I did eventually outgrow the worst of that and not so long ago scored no mean accolade, dubbed 'a good patient' by one of my son's colleagues doing root canal work.

The pivotal point. Its next star appearance in my life was as the exact place where the Roche family lived. Foreigners dwelling at the heart of our hometown. No 'Johnny Foreigners' these, much less 'bloody foreigners': they were well-liked and respected neighbours, thoroughly 'integrated', to use today's parlance. The hero of the Maginot Line and his English kith and kin. His nephew Godfrey was a pal of mine; sometimes I would call on him and we'd go for a stroll and a chat. In one such conversation I remarked, 'I never tell lies' – surely the mother of all whoppers – I wonder if George Washington ever indulged in similar 'inexactitudes'.

The pivotal point. At that precise location one day – I must have been eight or nine – I chanced to come face-to-face with Mr Sims, our headmaster. But I didn't say 'Good morning' or 'Hello' or in any way acknowledge his presence. The reason was embarrassment, as it often is for things otherwise inexplicable, coupled with confusion. How to address him? 'Sir?' 'Mr Sims'? And what else if anything should I say? 'How are you?' 'Have a nice day' hadn't been thought up yet. Uncertain, embarrassed, confused, I opted for silence.

In response he in turn said nothing, and went on his way. But he rightly thought he should give me a lesson and came specially to the classroom next day to do so. Never again did I ignore him, or any other acquaintance at a chance meeting.

I wish he'd given me more of such lessons – on how to behave, how to cope with social situations that catch one on the back foot. How to live, in fact. I've never been over-endowed with common sense; things that people who are so endowed take in their stride often floor me. Throughout the years, I've needed all the guidance I could get about handling everyday life – for me, as a challenge, it out-everests Everest by several thousand feet.

Mr Sims couldn't have known all that, but he did understand: his role as a teacher concerned not just academic matters but life in general. He would sometimes pop in and dispense this or that item of knowledge – some of it connected with school subjects, much of it not. One instance I particularly recall: drawing our attention to the fact that breathing is involuntary, he said, 'We don't have to remind ourselves continually, breathe, breathe, or else you'll die.'

Science was his domain, as the BSc added to his signature on our reports testified. Did he have any inkling that some of us were cut out to pursue a similar career? None more so than Rosemary; she had much talent for science (as well as for the arts, and had a hard time choosing between them before entering sixth form). She was destined to go not only as far as but much further than our esteemed headmaster – in the field of molecular biology, it so happened. In fact she was the stuff of which Nobels are made – I would never have been surprised if she'd gone on to be so recognised. But, as mentioned elsewhere, she relinquished all that in favour of social work aimed at building a new 'Jerusalem/In England's green and pleasant land'. To the dismay of some of her friends – including me – but she thought that was the right thing to do so, for her, I suppose it was.

Rosemary figures too in another 'pivotal point' event, neither the last nor the least of them. When, after the 'fair to end all fairs' and the more-than-a-mile trek home, my bladder started playing me up. Step by writhing step I was wondering how I'd make it without wetting my pants. Precisely at the pivotal point I feared I couldn't hold out a nano-second longer so, breaking away from my friend and her ever-present Mama, I made a hobbling dash for our stone's-throw-off loo. Blessed relief!

Memories are indeed made of this – how suitable, nay, serendipitous, that so many of mine are sign-posted, as it were, by that truly centre-stage spot.

None more so than this last one – the last and anything but the least. When we were riding in Granddad's cortège on his final journey (from 301 to 709, the number of his resting place shared with Granny) at that very place, the pivotal point, we espied a lout who offered no sign of respect – to Albert Rodwell, one of the town's most exemplary citizens. He who never omitted to grant the deceased their due, never failing to show any passing funeral proper regard, removing his hat in deference – as I'd observed countless times since my early infancy, on our walks about town together.

How shocked I was! How hurt! I wondered whether Granddad was aware of this shameful lapse and, if so, what his reaction was.

Tolerance and forgiveness, I'm sure. For he who always honoured the dead was always unstinting in forbearance and compassion towards the living. Never withholding anything that was in his power to give – including, often enough, sheer help in the form of any asset at his command.

I don't know who that lout was – what sort of person – 'common' or 'posh' or whatever. That's irrelevant. Granddad would have forgiven him, regardless, with a benign 'never mind'.

It is salutary to be reminded of that last journey, that sad day in September 1950, as I am reminded whenever I catch sight on the map of that truly pivotal point, that very heart of our beloved town.

Bags

His name was Mr Gascoigne. Rosemary it was who dreamed up for him the soubriquet 'Bags', after the manner of Cockney rhyming slang: Gascoigne – gas-bags – bags. I don't know for certain whether he knew of this or not but my guess is he did. I think teachers usually know what their pupils are saying about them: by one route or another, it filters through. On the other hand, pupils don't always know everything their teachers are saying about them; that grapevine is more closely guarded.

Bags was probably 'the best teacher I ever had' – if there has to be such a title – but why should there? No need. Still, if some contest were held for it, he'd be one of the strongest contenders, maybe the frontrunner.

He was our form master in the top class at Cranborne – 1A. There we were seniors, like sixth formers in secondary schools: guys the others are expected to look up to, sometimes resented and/or envied. 'Prefects' equals 'privileged'. However, the moment such top-graders move on – from elementary school to secondary, or from sixth form to beginners in some job, they immediately revert to being the juniorest of the junior. At any rate, for our appointed spell, basking in that aura of high rank, we queened it over the rest of Cranborne – and thoroughly enjoyed queening it. Under the joint aegis of Bags and Mr Sims the Head, twin custodians of our brief reign of glory. Afterwards I learned that the two of them declared there'd never been a 1A like ours, either before or since. There was, they recognised, something quite exceptional about it. I wonder, exactly what? Perhaps the way we were receptive, like no other, to the marvellous tutelage they gave. And of those two 'custodians', Bags of course was the closer to us; *plus intime*, in our presence day in, day out, month after month, all through those magic terms of '40 and '41. While the Head occasionally popped in to dispense some gem of enlightenment, Bags was the one giving guidance non-stop and frequently no mean gems of his own.

I recall so many instances of this; I'll cite just one or two. The first concerned our forays into literature. It may seem odd that we made the acquaintance of Cervantes before that of Shakespeare. But there was a good reason for that. We had to 'do' Don Quixote working from an abridged translation, whereas we'd have had to swallow the Bard neat – a bit too much to ask of ten or eleven-year-olds. Before we embarked on the exploits of the hidalgo, Bags gave us a choice: would we like to pronounce his name the Spanish or the English way? The fact that we unanimously opted for the Spanish showed just how broad-minded was that favourite 1A of theirs. In passing, it may be noted that our tolerance of things Spanish pleasantly offset a picture on our classroom wall, 'The Boyhood of Raleigh', in which an old salt in the Devon countryside is pointing out to the hero-to-be, the sea and the far distant Spanish main: the challenge of an enemy as daunting in those Elizabethan days as Hitler was in ours.

Another striking memory of Bags – one day we came back from our lunch break to find the blackboard filled to overflowing with fascinating drawings, done by Bags himself, illustrating a new project we were to launch into that afternoon. To produce these pictures – so well drawn, in such a lot of detail – he must have sacrificed his own lunch break, plus maybe putting his feet up in the staff room – (don't teachers spend most of their working hours on their feet?) – even a forty winks or so. A sacrifice I'm sure he was only too glad to make. His efforts hit us in the eye the instant we entered the classroom, firing our curiosity and whetting our appetite. Talk about 'over and above the call of duty'. He didn't have to do all that; we could have just started the project without preamble. But he wanted us to be intrigued, enjoy it to the full, and give it our best.

Bags' tour de force was perhaps his Friday afternoon 'treat' – we looked forward to that all week. It comprised free periods when we could do our thing without let or hindrance. For us, acting it had to be. We ran a sort of soap. Henry and Maria were the names of the husband-and-wife leads; Rosemary and I took turns as Maria but Henry was always played by Douglas Freeman – one of the top boys, sitting in the same row with Derek Stockbridge. (I heard eventually that he became a priest – or clergyman was it?) He had great fun in Henry mode, especially in one episode when he was knocked out by Maria and lay supine under Bags' desk, chuckling the while. I don't recall the plots of any of these 'mini-series' (any more than those of the playgames with Marion). But did we have fun acting them! (Bags of course 'directing'.) The audience too – I've no doubt it made their week. The not-so-clever ones – non-crème-de-la-crème though they were, even they enjoyed and benefited a great deal from these wonderful Fridays. It strikes me that it was a bit of luck for them being part of that star-studded 1A some of its glamour must have rubbed off on them, whether they liked it or not!

I have no doubt that Rosemary and I, together with our dear comrade Margaret Wood, were Bags's favourites. Though he strove to be fair to all his charges (totalling about thirty, the norm in those days) all too naturally he would often gravitate towards us, closeted in our élite corner – kids were seated according to rated cleverness. There, he could expect some intelligent discussion, up to if not better than what was available in the staff room. Some feedback to his ideas. He'd provide feedback to ours too.

Not always agreement. Once he ticked Rosemary off for a remark she made to James Bentley (only a 'moderately clever') whom we tended to exclude from our list of possible friends (or the cast of our soap for that matter). I don't like to put this on record – but was our discrimination because he was a little on the dark side? A tad 'coloured'? What some people referred to as 'a touch of the tarbrush?' (That accusation was frequently levelled at Mrs Simpson and was possibly the main reason why she could never be accepted as queen). Practically everyone those days, from Churchill down, was racist, to a lesser or greater degree, and we in the enlightened 1A were no exceptions. But Bags really was above all that. I could see he was sorry for James and tried to make amends for our cold-shouldering him – hoping, perhaps, we'd outgrow it. Or that, somehow James (he was after all a nice guy) would eventually win us over. Well, whatever the reason, he was nothing like in the same league as Derek, John Morris or Douglas Freeman.

Bags especially appreciated – and, I guess, keenly awaited – our weekly set compositions. More often than not, Rosemary's or mine got the highest marks. But on one occasion he judged Margaret's to be far superior to mine and marked them accordingly. He felt he had to justify this to me – indicating this and that, drawing my attention to where she'd done so much better. 'You do see my point don't you?' And I did. He was definitely right, hers was certainly the better of the two. Again, he didn't have to do all that – he could have just handed the papers back, duly marked, without comment. But it seemed he thought I merited an apology.

Sometimes the set subjects were a doddle; others harder to get our teeth into. 'Autobiography of a Carthorse' was one I found tough going – but at least it taught us what 'autobiography' meant.

When the fateful day arrived for us to leave Cranborne, we put on a show, inviting the whole school and several of us did turns. One of our classmates, Tony Glover, was a good comedian and his number brought the house down. As for Rosemary and me, we essayed some slapstick stuff – but we were no good! By rights we should have been booed off stage! But on the contrary, we got loads of applause: supposedly because our hearts were so obviously in it, the whole school warmed to us. And even if I went red in the face or my facial nerve twitched I didn't care – what the hell! The climax of the show was when we presented farewell gifts to our beloved mentors; Mr Sims and Bags. I don't think any 1A before or since outdid us in any of this. No wonder we were the favourites. Never to be forgotten.

It cut both ways. Forget? Impossible. Here am I, almost seventy years later, reliving and relishing every instant of those wonderful times.

It's a corny old truism that 'schooldays are the best days of our lives' and more often than not it's a lie. But for me, as far as Cranborne was concerned, it was absolutely true. Thanks to all those splendid teachers throughout the six years – from Miss Gower, the vicar's daughter from South Mimms, who took me in with the youngest of the infants, to the Head himself. It wasn't only that they were dedicated and talented: they were excellently trained too. This is very obvious to me now, looking back. You hear so much nowadays about how standards have gone down, how thousands of eleven-year-olds are unable to read. How on earth? Whatever has gone wrong? I'm just flabbergasted. In our day, you simply couldn't help but learn; culture and knowledge rubbed of on you – whether you liked it or not. Even those also-rans, the non-crème-de-la-crème. They got by. More than just satisfactorily. No one could help being on the receiving end of the treasures so generously supplied, by all of those mentors – none more so than Bags. He gave us all he'd got and that was one hell of a lot.

My final memory of him is the greatest. On my last report he wrote, 'Well done, top girl!'

I showed this to Rosemary, who by a very narrow margin, had come second. I knew she wouldn't mind.

She'd share my happiness, and she did. Though her Ma was a little peeved: she tended to view us as rivals, each keen to out-do the other, which wasn't the case at all. As for Margaret Wood, she too was unselfishly pleased for me, and for Rosemary – never was there a more gracious recipient of bronze.

As for me, I can't adequately describe the feeling Bags' words gave me. I don't think any other accolade whatsoever could have given me more joy – not even a PhD.

Riding Down from Bangor

Riding down from Bangor
on an eastern train
after weeks of hunting
in the woods of Maine
Quite extensive whiskers,
Beard, moustache as well
Sat a student fellow
Tall and slim and swell
Empty seat beside him
no one at his side
into rural station
eastern train did glide
Enter aged couple
Take the hindmost seat
Enter village maiden –
Beautiful, petite…

And so on and so forth. There are umpteen verses. This was one of our favourite songs in the Holiday Fellowship song book; we used to belt it out often and regularly over the years.

Holiday Fellowship was a club Doris belonged to, along with several of her friends. The group travelled a lot together including, pre-war, a trip to Switzerland.

They had great fun. Not only in this area but in general. I am constantly impressed by this fact – that generation had fun, despite the overwhelming tragedy of WWI, and the many difficulties that beset them – especially financial ones; the Depression. And the constant threat of serious health problems. They had fun and it shows – it streams out of those old sepia photos, how they were enjoying life to the full. Strikingly – perhaps most striking of all were those women who lost their loved menfolk in the war yet went on to live rich, fulfilling lives, single. None was more typical of this than Doris's close friend Lalla Scruby, who, among many other accomplishments, sang in choirs under Dr Malcolm Sargent – she who took me to the Vic Oliver show as a reward for my passing 'matric' – and treated me as an equal, discussing problems with me, respecting my opinions.

In various areas of life, that generation had a great deal more fun than my own – (or at least than me personally. Joie de vivre has never been my strong suit – melancholic, that's me). There's no comparison.

Take for example Mummy, Doris and Elsie and her husband Jack, plus of course Daddy, and Sid with his great chum Jack Hawkins (of 'Bridge on the River Kwai' fame), having fun as teenagers and young adults – acting, singing, Gilbert and Sullivaning. Gathered around the piano in Edwardian days, giving it all they'd got, in chorus or solo. No one has written more movingly about this than DH Lawrence; in the poem telling how as a child he clung to his mother's skirts as she played the piano and they all sang – and how, remembering it he 'wept like a child for the past'. This poem also underlines how everyone learned the piano way back then; everyone had a piano, the poor as well as the comfortably off. People then provided ample entertainment for themselves. It was DIY and it went on for decades – through all the interwar years right up to WWII and beyond.

The Holiday Fellowship song book was just one proof of all this. It was quite hefty and reposed under the lift-up seat of the piano stool, along with other sheet music – much of the repertoire of Sims Reeves, Lotte Lehman and other stars of Edwardian and late Victorian vintage. All this focus on music, on making your own music, symbolised the triumphant lifestyle of our parents' generation – and preceding ones too. Triumphant, yes – I use that word advisedly. They indeed triumphed, sensationally, over 'things'.

But back to 'Riding Down from Bangor'. I don't know why it was our favourite but it was. With its countless verses. I've forgotten most of them but one in particular was so memorable and meaningful for me. It goes like this:

Whizz, slap, bang!
Into tunnel quite
Into glorious darkness
Black as Egypt's night

Now why should Egypt's night be blacker than that of any other country? (Now if they'd said 'black as Cleopatra's wigs' it would have made sense). But why mention Egypt anyway? And why on earth should we be singing this month after month, year after year, there in 301? Completely unaware that Egypt was the land where I was destined to spend by far the greater part of my life. Egypt – it was out there, waiting for me, so to speak, all through the '30s and '40s. Waiting. Yet we didn't know.

Though there were pointers; pointers galore. Though we didn't recognise them as such when they happened. Like 'I've fallen in the arabus' – the very first words I ever addressed to my mother (assuming – as seems likely – that I never visited her when she was hospitalised) when she finally rejoined me on my fourth birthday, having left me when I was three months old.

Then there was the remarkable 'Sahara desert' pointer. When, strolling around Kensington with a very close friend I asked him, 'Where do you think I'll spend the rest of my life?' and he answered, 'Why, here in London, of course. Where do you think? In the Sahara desert?'

And most impressive of all, the illustration in my Bible, and its maps showing Egypt, Alexandria and Arabia, as well as Libya, Benghazi and Cyrenaica – all to become intrinsic parts of my future – becoming, eventually, as familiar to me as Mutton Lane and Forestdale. Those images were in front of me, facing me day after day as I sat through Scripture lessons in Cranborne, and week after week as I took part in Sunday school sessions under the Rev. Aubrey Argyll DD – yet I never had an inkling, 'That's where I'm going, that's where I'll finally settle. That's where my nearest and dearest will come from. That's what mapped out for me.'

Even when I became so absorbed in Caesar and Cleopatra and all things Ptolemaic – I saw the Gabriel Pascal film of Shaw's play seven times – even then I didn't 'foresee' my coming Egyptian life.

And no one else did either, when I used to spend all my Saturdays with Daddy, at 301 or traipsing around Potters Bar, listening to Churchill's speeches pouring out of people's open windows – or at Southgate, watching the football in Broomfield Park – never did I dream that the last time I'd ever see Daddy would be at Cairo Airport or the last outing we'd ever do together would be to El Alamein.

But back to Bangor. The saga of that 'eastern train'. Wouldn't you like to know what happened to that quartet of passengers?

Pleasantly they chatted:
How the cinders fly!'
Till the student fellow
Gets one in the eye.
Maiden sympathetic
Turns herself about.
'May I if you please, sir,
Try to get it out?'

Now, look out, here it comes:

Whizz, slap, bang!
Into tunnel quite
Into glorious darkness
Black as Egypt's night.

Finally the dénouement:

Out into the sunshine – [
White as England's day?]
Glides the eastern train
Students' hair is ruffled
Just the merest grain.
Maiden seen all blushes
When then and there appeared
A tiny little earring
In that horrid student's beard.

Holidays at Home

There were several mottos hammered into our brains throughout the war on posters, in the press, on the wireless. Careless talk costs lives', 'Is your journey really necessary?', 'Make do and mend' – these were among the more depressing. But there was one that had a very positive impact and that was 'Holidays at Home'. Made you think, 'Why not?' After all, it was either that or no holidays, period. That is, if it was the seaside you were hankering after, always most people's preference. The coast was declared off-limits 'for the duration', for security reasons. It included of course Bognor, in Sussex, our family's favourite for the annual break, ever since I was a toddler. Let's give it its proper name, Bognor Regis, conferred on it because the royal family, sharing our preference, spent their vacations there several summers in a row. However, the King himself (George-V) wasn't as enamoured of the place as his wife and children were – if we are to believe the anecdote about his 'famous last words'. As he lay bedridden during his final illness, Queen Mary tried to cheer him up. 'Never mind, dear, as soon as you're better we can go to Bognor!' To which his somewhat unregal response was, 'Bugger Bognor!'

Holidays at home. Not a bad idea at all. Bearing in mind that sometimes surrogates are better than the real thing. We were all in favour of it – but wondering about the nitty-gritty. Where exactly to go and what to do once we got there? Stately homes weren't everyone's cup of tea and we'd already visited most of them in our 'catchment area'. Answers to our queries didn't materialise till our Southgate phase, i.e. starting 1941.

Southgate – leafy suburb that it is. Not enough having beautifully tree-lined streets, with cherry blossoms rivalling those of Japan – ask Mr Fujihito, our neighbour a few doors along; he should know. But in addition boasting no less than four big parks – Grovelands, Arnos, Oakwood and Broomfield. Of these, Broomfield was the most interesting, its history going back a few centuries. Broomfield House, at the centre of the park, was there in Tudor times and so were the famous elms. This avenue of splendid trees ran from the vicinity of the House right up to the park's northernmost entrance at the top of Alderman's Hill – of which Forestdale is virtually a continuation, serving not only residential purposes (for the likes of us) but acting as a short cut between Broomfield and Arnos Park (and the adjacent Underground station, Arnos Grove). So living in Forestdale, we were spoilt for choice; with all this on our doorstep, no excuse for not having 'Holidays at Home'.

Broomfield House was also the original location of Southgate County School (where I followed in my father's footsteps); he was enrolled there pre-1914, with his friends the Finlayson brothers whose names appear with many others of that generation on the roll of honour commemorating the fallen of WWI. A sad aspect of the place's history.

Broomfield was so much more than an ordinary park. It had all the usual amenities: roundabouts and swings, tennis courts and a football pitch – Daddy and I would often linger there of a Saturday afternoon watching the game – he kept up his weekend visits to me unfailingly, just as when I was at Potters Bar. He was a lifelong supporter of Tottenham Hotspur and naturally I inherited this allegiance, 'Up the Spurs!'

But there were other features at Broomfield besides the sport-geared ones. A big greenhouse à la Kew, and opposite the House itself, three beautiful ponds, miniature lakes, with varied flora and fauna. Plus – its most memorable asset, I thought – a garden for the blind, based on the scents of plants, from which the sighted too could benefit to their heart's content.

I often used to rush through Broomfield, the quickest way from Forestdale to Palmers Green Public Library where, with a bit of luck, I might find my other grandfather – Granddad Thomas Freshwater Briggs, as ardent a bibliophile as I was, even then, and we would have a lovely time browsing together. Other readers we might bump into included Stevie Smith, the Palmers Green poet, and Flora Robson, our locally resident film star.

It is distressing to relate that both the House and the Park have in recent years fallen on hard times, as a result of a series of accidents. The House has been reduced to a travesty of its former self, and the Elm Avenue has disappeared, recalling those lines of Cowper, 'The poplars are felled; farewell to the shade and the whispering sound of the cool colonnade'. Efforts to resuscitate both Park and House with all their treasures have been pursued actively by a dedicated group of enthusiasts, even to the extent of seeking for Broomfield national heritage status. So far these have not succeeded but the campaign continues, undiscouraged, and I certainly hope it eventually achieves its aim.

In our schooldays of the early '40s, however, both House and Park were in their heyday, forming an ideal venue for Holidays at Home. I presume there must have been consultations at local government level about this; schools were an obvious source of good suggestions. Accordingly it came about that Southgate County was asked to be responsible for the first major attraction – and the best, it so turned out. Nothing less than a Shakespeare play. And which of his plays are more suitable for a summer entertainment than *A Midsummer Night's Dream*? Starring the most gifted actors among our schoolmates, and directed by the most multi-talented of our teachers, Mrs Pole. She wore other hats too – her day-job, one might call it, was as senior French teacher, and she was also swimming instructor. But masterminding school theatricals was where she shone at her very brightest.

Staged on the lawns by the lakes, facing the House, this performance proved to be a 'Dream' of a lifetime. In fact I can honestly say it was the most memorable Shakespeare production I've ever seen – including one with Laurence Olivier and Vivien Leigh. I'm not kidding. And I'm sure the Bard himself would not have been displeased by it. Casting was brilliant – and Mrs Pole knew it. Her satisfaction with her chosen thespians showed. 'Isn't he handsome!' she enthused about her Theseus. But the undoubted stars were her Oberon and Puck. The former had a balletic presence you could fairly say out-Nureyeved Nureyev in sheer exotic glamour. And as for the Puck, surely those lines:

Thou speak'st aright;
I am that merry wanderer of the night!

could never have been better rendered, even at the Globe.

The whole experience was simply unforgettable. Even nowadays, when I'm exchanging letters with friends of those years and mention any of our colleagues who took part in that Dream, we identify them by the roles they played in it. As in 'You know, my cousin Beryl, she was Pease Blossom' and 'I met Betty Thackeray the other day – Titania, remember?'

Superb as it all was, amateur is always amateur, with an informality you'll never get from pros – but that only added to the charm. When, for example, Hermia was asked, 'Why is thy cheek so pale?' while her rouge was redder than red, prompting shrieks of laughter – a bonus you'd never get on Shaftesbury Avenue. Yes, we sure had our 'Holidays at Home', without even having to travel to the West End.

Though this was the undisputed jewel in the Broomfield crown, other entertainments were laid on over the next few years – in fact right up till the war came to an end in 1945. It was almost a shame when the embargo on the coast was lifted and we could all go again to Bognor, or wherever fancy dictated – and bid farewell to those intriguing home-made 'surrogates'.

It was certainly a relief not be exhorted any longer to 'make do and mend'. However, some of those slogans have acquired a new relevance nowadays. 'Is your journey really necessary?' particularly so: now we are urged to curtail our CO^2 footprints; now we are being lectured (with just as much reason as before, if not more): most of our proposed journeys could be seen not only as unnecessary but as downright acts of sabotage. In the next war – is it to be WWIII? Not against terrorists but climate change and global warming – enemies more insidious than Hitler but just as harmful. If, and when, such a war gets underway – it hasn't had its 3rd September yet, let alone its 11th September – there won't be much scope for 'Holidays at Home'. There may well be not only no holidays but no home either – if what we mean by home is Planet Earth.

Omar Khayyam

Vic Oliver – Der Old Vic – wasn't the only one of our favourite personalities who had strong links with Johannesburg. Vic, as mentioned in an earlier piece, ended his days there, in the dressing room of a theatre – what more fitting end for one whose life had been devoted to entertaining the public? But there was someone else, in Potters Bar itself, whose great love was South Africa – he hailed from there and confided that, when the time came, he wanted his ashes scattered over that very city – Jo'burg.

This was a leading figure in our lives, Mr Ralston, dentist neighbour of Dr Porter, our GP, the 'laughing gas' guru. They dwelt side by side, their two houses forming part of a trio, a little way up Mutton Lane from us. Two houses one dreaded to visit. As for the third – I wonder who lived there. Someone unknown, who inspired no fear – and no love either. Like a non-person in a non-home.

Throughout our life in Potters Bar we never went to any other dentist, though there were several in town. Even after I moved to live week-days at the Kensington convent (to be nearer my work place, Harrods) I would always go to Mutton Lane to let Mr Ralston attend to my teeth. And boy did they need attending to! Largely due to my penchant for chocolate, rationed or unrationed.

Between ourselves, Mother and I didn't call him Mr Ralston, but Omar Khayyam. Doubtless inspired by a certain look about him; he could 'pass as' a fair-skinned Arab or indeed a Persian, though he didn't look un-English either. One of those people who fit in comfortably across quite a broad ethnic spectrum.

Our giving him this alias shows how well known Omar Khayyam was and had been for decades in England; he had secured an unassailable niche in our culture. Thanks very largely of course to Fitzgerald's translation – which had struck exactly the right note for an English readership. In Harrods Book Department I couldn't fail to notice how popular the 'Rubaiyat' was, perennial bestseller; more people bought it than any other book and after Shakespeare it was the most widely read and quoted.

Though over the years we got to know Mr Ralston well, we never let on to him about this alias. But perhaps he guessed!

He was a very conscientious practitioner as well as very efficient. I have a difficult set of teeth and he had to do a lot of surgery on them. They were already in a delicate condition and he told me to bear this in mind when presenting myself to others for future treatment. 'Fragile, handle with care!'

It was through him that I first realised that one's relationship with one's dentist can be exceptionally close. Inescapably locked in his embrace, so to speak, confidences are inevitable. Even though the patient can't, physically, speak for much of the time – never mind, sometimes a few affirmative, sympathetic grunts suffice as conversation. Like with hairdressers, or taxi-drivers – closeted together, the rest of the world shut out, you simply have to relate to each other. Either party may seize the chance to open up – 'Open wide'! – about matters currently preoccupying them.

I was reminded of this recently by 'The Yacoubian Building', bestseller produced by Cairo dentist Alaa El Aswany. I'm not surprised that despite his literary success, he's not giving up dentistry – his patients being a prime source of material for his books.

Way back in those Mutton Lane days I could hardly have foreseen that dentistry would play a big role in my family life too, since my son Aly chose it as his career and his wife and daughters likewise. On that score alone, I'm often reminded of Mr Ralston. But there's an even more powerful reason for remembering him. I ask myself – was it one of those uncanny indicators of the future when Mother dubbed him 'Omar Khayyam'? Since our first little son, who lived only twenty days, we called 'Omar'.

WASPS, where is Your Sting?

Of course, Potters Bar wasn't inhabited exclusively by White Anglo Saxon Protestants, though naturally they did comprise the overwhelming majority. In those days there were absolutely no blacks in town – a single one would have stood out like a sore thumb. I'm pretty sure that now it's totally different and that, demographically speaking, things have changed enormously over the fifty years since I left.

In the '30s and '40s it was freely acknowledged that a 'colour bar' (a term much used then) not only existed but flourished. Furthermore, we all admitted, albeit among ourselves, to being 'prejudiced' (this word too was much bandied about) to a lesser or greater degree. Conspiratorially whispering 'Aren't we awful!' – most of us had the decency to be shamefaced about it. But conspiratorial, confidential or not, the phenomenon was quite observable, plainly there, for all the world to see. When, for instance, someone only slightly darker than olive-skinned applied for a bedsit to be told firmly, 'No coloureds' – with or without 'sorry'.

However, when on the odd occasion such a person did make the grade, they did so in a big way – securing not only the acceptance of the native WASPs but their admiration. Indeed, not only admired, but lionised, becoming a species of mascot. This happened mainly in the realms of sport or entertainment. An outstanding example was Paul Robeson, who virtually had a monopoly on 'Ol' Man River'; few other singers would dare attempt a rendition of what was viewed as his song. Another such 'mascot' was Leary Constantine, a doughty cricketer from the subcontinent.

Making the grade did occur too, though very rarely, in more mundane walks of life. And there again, when it did happen, it happened big. One instance of this was a doctor who for a short while practised in the Chase Road area of Southgate. He wasn't just more than olive-skinned – he was black with a capital B. Yet the èlite and the would-be èlite of the leafy suburb vied jealously to be on his panel. Just why I'll never fathom. Perhaps because he was very handsome, à la Sidney Poitier, or had loads of sex appeal. Anyway, he provided striking evidence of an exception to the rule.

In Potters Bar there was what might be described as a borderline case: a much – sought-after obstetrician. He himself was WASP – white – but his wife – wait for it – was Egyptian. I never met her so I'm not sure about her complexion – in Egypt a whole gamut of skin colour prevails. However that may be, posh and would-be posh expectant mothers flocked in droves to be delivered by her husband. And by the way furnishing another pointer to the link between Potters Bar and Egypt – a link which Timmy, alias me, was destined to forge to no mean degree.

It may be noted here that the people of my hometown were quite well informed about the situation prevailing then in Egypt (and many other lands in that vast 'other' that we call 'abroad').Thanks to the forerunners of the tabloids. We were kept especially well-briefed about the doings of royalty – perhaps they were seen as colleagues, or confrères, of our own highly adulated top family. Not only the princely ones of such countries as Belgium, Holland, and Sweden but those further afield, e.g. Thailand (then of course called Siam – vide Anna and the King thereof). And yes, too, Egypt. Thus in my childhood we and our neighbours knew the basic facts about the reigning dynasty there; when I was only about eight I learned that everyone in that family was required to have a name beginning with F or N. Hence King Farouk, his father King Fouad, his mother Queen Nazli, and his sisters Princesses Fawzia, Fathia, Faiza and Fawia. As well as his wives: firstly Queen Farida then Queen Narriman. King Farouk himself was much admired in England then, and sympathetically presented in the media. A handsome young man, he often enhanced cinema newsreels and the pages of such papers as *The People* on Sunday and the *Daily Sketch*. (A tabloid by any other name). While at the same time many of his 'subjects' were being routinely turned away at countless European bedsits. Which shows, when it comes to race – and quite a lot besides – it helps more than a little to be royal. *Plus ça change.*

Faith, Hope and Verity

In the late 1930s Uncle Sid was prosperous, 'a stockbroker, doing well'. All that changed as a result of the war, in which he served in the RAF, and he had to adapt to a much less affluent lifestyle. This he did with great dignity and good humour. But way back then, he could afford luxuries the rest of the family couldn't (though he lavished a lot of them on us). For example, unlike the majority of our class, he could splurge on cruises abroad, and of course he had a car – he loved driving and often took us on outings. He also had a billiards table (where Pat and his brothers used to play) and a fridge – hardly anyone had one those days – in the poshly appointed kitchen which Vi, his wife, thoroughly deserved, as she was a superlative cook. Her charlotte russe, her pièce de résistance, was renowned throughout the neighbourhood and beyond. She had, too, another unheard-of luxury for our class – a maid living in. The girl was called Verity. She and I – a frequent visitor – got on very well.

One day it was decided she could take me to the cinema – the Odeon in Southgate. (Strictly speaking, Uncle's home was in Enfield West, as Oakwood used to be called). A Robert Donat film was showing (no one called them 'movies' then) – *The Ghost Goes West*. It was about a Scottish castle transported brick-by-brick across the Atlantic, complete with resident ghost. Sounded fascinating. So, Verity and I duly set out on a very long walk: the entire length of Chase Road. Talk about 'as long as Oxford Street' – I guess it's a good deal longer, probably the longest residential road in UK.

The film must indeed have fulfilled our expectations, as, instead of vacating our seats when it ended and starting out on the homeward trek, we decided to sit it through a second time. It never occurred to either of us that we should pay again or – more seriously – that the family would be worried stiff about our not getting back in proper time. We did in fact leave the cinema and start on our way home just before a notice about us was flashed on the screen – that would have put the skids under us all right.

It was, I suppose, my fault but it was reprehensible of Verity to encourage me. She after all was the adult, the responsible one, and shouldn't have given in to me. Perhaps she thought of me, employers' relative that I was, as a sort of boss? But she – and me too for that matter – should have realised how extremely anxious they'd all be. After all, even I knew that Potters Bar had its share of killers and other criminals (see 'How not to earn five bob'); I should have realised that Southgate too might well have its quota.

Verity got a severe reprimand when we at last turned up at No 42, Chase Road. If she'd been sacked it wouldn't have been unreasonable. But apart from this she'd given good service, so they kept her on rather than engaging a replacement from the agency that had supplied her. Previous applicants from there interviewed by Vi had had names like Mercy, Modesty, Faith – I believe it drew its recruits from a convent orphanage.

Incidentally, I haven't seen a Robert Donat film in ages. A big star in his day, of course he's well documented in the annals, but many cinema-goers today have never even heard of him. A shame. He was a first-class pro and I was an ardent fan. *The Ghost Goes West*. I certainly wouldn't mind seeing it again. I can't remember the story, but it must have been superb entertainment, to have kept us riveted to our seats for about five hours.

Wireless Icons

I wonder where we'd have put the TV if we'd had one. Probably on the cabinet that formed part of the Chewdless Hairdressing Salon. Thus depriving Bimby, my senior imaginary friend, with his carving-embellished fortress.

As for those other features then lurking in the future, the fridge of course would have gone in the 'larder' (nowadays already a little-used word, let's say obsolescent). The computer would belong in the as-yet-to-be-installed study in the loft. The car? Parked on the Verge, keeping the fire hydrant company – we would never have knocked down the Gathorne – inscribed gate to let it on to our home ground proper.

With TV going full blast, with reality shows and the like, Mummy would have found it hard to concentrate on her knitting let alone her 'Nursing Mirror'. Instead of the seductive crooning of Bryan Lawrence – the perfect background to her hobbies of nursing and knitting – eminently practical and useful like most of what she did. In fact in many ways she was the exact opposite of me, 'Iris isn't practical' being one of her bang on-target verdicts on her then sole offspring. I had loads in common with each of my aunts, Doris and Elsie – three sisters, even Chekhov's, could rarely have been less of a likeness. No matter, that's irrelevant. Here we're talking about TV. We didn't have it, no one did, and I doubt if we'd have opted for it even if we could have, instead of or in addition to our beloved wireless.

Perhaps I should mention here that just before the war, 1937ish, I went with Granddad to visit a Bowling Club mate who actually had acquired this novelty – I was duly fascinated and impressed. But it fizzled out just when the Munich crisis fizzled in – the time for it simply wasn't ripe.

Our beloved wireless far from being a non-must was something we couldn't live without. Its stars are well remembered to this twenty-first-century day – not only Bryan and his confrères, Dorothy Carless et al. Many of those artists had slots of their own, or they were mainstays of regular shows such as Children's

Hour of which I was a devotee for several years. The Zoo Man was my favourite, along with his side-kicks Larry the Lamb and Dennis the Daschund. As I grew up my focus of interest naturally shifted, to other programmes such as The Brains Trust featuring philosopher CEM Joad (our home-grown Socrates) and more especially Dr Malcolm Sargent, the very eminent conductor. (Around this time he was knighted but I always felt 'Dr' was a more distinguished handle than 'Sir'.) This debating forum comprised a foursome; the others were Julian Huxley and Commander Campbell, the latter voicing on the whole less intellectual, more common sense viewpoints. Among the many stimulating subjects chewed over was Joad's contention that many activities were more enjoyable than sex – an example he cited was eating chocolate peppermint creams. (Did Socrates ever make similar assertions? Xantippe* might have provoked them!) *Well, what do you know?* thought seventeen-year-old me. I'd not yet obtained much of a clue about sex, but I did have a pile of peppermint creams right there in front of me and I thought – if sex wasn't as pleasurable as those, what was the big deal? Incidentally, I'd got them with my sweets coupons; in 1947 rationing was still in force and I thought maybe there should also be coupons for sex, so everyone would be guaranteed their fair share – no more and no less!

Joad had his own special catch-phrase, 'It depends what you mean by…' whatever topic was up for discussion, and we eagerly awaited his resorting to it in every edition of the show. By this technique he could easily persuade his audience of any argument he might choose to present, such as black equals white or vice versa.

Among other wireless stars were Doris Arnold, with her prototype classical request series, *These You Have Loved*. Top of those pops, as far as I was concerned, was Isobel Baillie, *prima donna assoluta* of the oratorio she often sang under Dr Sargent's baton. 'I know that my Redeemer liveth' was the aria most closely associated with her – you might call it her piece, much as '*Nessun dorma*' became Pavarotti's or 'You are my heart's delight' Richard Tauber's – to the extent that it seems almost indecent if other singers presume to render them. I was a fervent fan of La Baillie (though not particularly of oratorio per se) and once I tramped miles to hear her live. I wanted to see what she looked like – I doubt if I'd have done that if frequently regaled with TV images of her.

---

* In case you've forgotten, Socrates' wife famously addicted to nagging her spouse.

She was, and still is, one of the main figures that spring to my mind in the 'Are Men Superior to Women?' controversy. Along with Amy Johnson, Freya Stark, Edith Summerskill (to name but three, the list is endless) she embodied quintessential excellence, equal to whatsoever male counterpart.

Granddad too had his wireless icons, notably Mr Middleton the gardening expert and Sandy MacPherson who'd tackle on his organ any item requested. There were several other organists on air and, oddly, many of them were named Reginald. Aged eight or so, I thought this was a sort of title for that profession, like judges being called Mr Justice So and So.

Those were the days. Never to be recaptured. Like we can't go back to silent movies. But when we do occasionally catch a glimpse of them we recognise – yes that was something marvellous, irreplaceable, unique. In truth a very hard act to follow.

Moscow Dynamos

Both separately and in collaboration, Rosemary and I delighted in writing parodies. One of hers, on the many Russia-geared melodies and choruses we heard in the war years – of which "Cavalry of the Steppes" was the greatest – went like this:

Travel, travel the comrades' way,
Travel by night and travel by day.
Who goes there on Joe Stalin's way?
A camaraderie.

'Uncle Joe' was viewed as an unmitigated good guy those days. It was only long afterwards that we learned about the atrocities, the gulags and the samizdat, and all the horrors chronicled in the works of Solzhenetsin and Pasternak – why, we hadn't even yet heard of Dr Zhivago! What we had heard though, thoroughly dinned into us, was 'Uncle Joe can do no wrong' – any more than Franklin D. Roosevelt could. It was a case of 'UK, USA and USSR' (a current pop song) powerfully illustrated by that famous photo: the two of them sitting alongside Churchill at the Yalta Conference. Apprising Hitler in no uncertain language, 'This is what you're up against.'

At the height of that alliance, holy or unholy as you might view it, London hosted a visit from a leading Russian football team, the Moscow Dynamos. Coverage of this was on the news as I watched our Forestdale next-door neighbour (on the non-Jewish side), Mr Jones, trudging home from a hard day's slog at the office, via Arnos Grove Tube Station and Arnos Park. I've no doubt he was more than glad to tuck in to the evening meal prepared by Mrs Jones. I have no idea whether he was giving the Dynamos a thought – or whether he was a football fan or not. Anyway, in that non-TV era he wouldn't be able to agonise over every goal and penalty shoot-out – all the better to get on with his much-needed meal.

Talk about 'keeping up with the Joneses'! They couldn't have been more aptly named – quintessential London neighbours, they minded their own business and we minded ours, a nod of recognition being about all we'd exchange if we came face-to-face in the street.

But one day during our four-year stay in Southgate, the unthinkable happened and Ma actually went into Mrs Jones's kitchen. What warranted, or triggered, this unparalleled event remains unknown to this day. Perhaps barriers were indeed coming down without our knowing it. Psychological barriers – as real as the fence in which Mr Magnus had cut his historic gap. Even so, Granny and Granddad never once availed themselves of that gap, and Mrs Magnus never graced our kitchen with her presence. It would have been lovely if she had! However, whatever the reason, things were changing and Ma's epoch-making visit should have featured on the wireless, announced by star wartime anchors Alvar Liddell or Bruce Belfrage – every bit as 'breaking news' as the London match with the Dynamos.

Nowadays, of course, it's nothing for football teams to travel world-wide even for Chelsea to play Arsenal in Moscow. Doesn't make sense to me! Who benefits? Presumably the Russian 'oligarchs' (a new breed, and a new word, never heard of in Uncle Joe's time) who, preposterous as it may seem, actually own several UK clubs. Paying billions for the transfer of stars – and to the stars themselves. Billionaire slaves you might call them – how's that for an oxymoron?

Wasn't it far more fun, and far more sport, in those 'Cavalry of the Steppes' days? And when Yuri Gagarin went on his somewhat more than glob-trotting journeys. Wonder how much he got paid? (Not to mention Laika. In case you've forgotten, the Russian dog who pioneered their space travel.) Lucky if he cashed a few roubles.

By the way, don't know who won that match. Don't care!

The Guard's Chapel

On my fourteenth birthday, 1944, the war was entering its endgame and its ferocity, far from abating, was increasing markedly. Nonetheless, as far as possible, we tried to live up to our wartime maxim, 'Business as usual'.

This included going to the theatre. Daddy took me for a birthday treat to see *The Yeomen of the Guard*. Like many grand opera buffs – as I was rapidly becoming – I didn't like Gilbert and Sullivan, but *the Yeomen* was an exception. An added allure was that in the local (Southgate) production the lead role of Jack Point was played by none other than our much-admired maths master, Mr Armstrong.

It was fun to see him wearing a different hat. It was fun enough when he wore his usual, day-job one; it was always very entertaining to watch him solve maths problems mentally, reading them upside-down from the textbooks on our desks and producing the answers in the twinkling of an eye. He often sang in school concerts too – providing a role model for any of us kids to pluck up the guts to sing in public. I needed that kind of encouragement; I knew I had quite a nice voice but for years my wretched nerves stopped me from climbing up on stage and getting my stuff across.

Mr Armstrong was certainly multi-talented. And he wasn't lacking either in that *sine qua non* for all thespians, amateur or pro – adherence to their basic article of faith. Only Noël Coward, that man of the theatre par excellence, was allowed to question it, as he does in his famous song, 'Why must the show go on?'

We duly turned up at *The Yeomen* and were enjoying the performance when, about half-way through, the air-raid siren sounded. Not the slightest flicker of awareness was visible from those on stage and the show did indeed go on – in the highest tradition, worthy of Coward himself. So we in the audience also stayed put.

That incident passed without mishap but next day, Sunday, it was a very different matter. One of the most remembered, and most notorious, London raids happened – a direct hit on the Guards' Chapel in the heart of town. It struck in the middle of the morning service; there were many casualties. This military house of worship has been for centuries, and still is, the scene of countless royal and national occasions – such as, quite recently, a memorial ceremony for Princess Diana. It is a national institution, a veritable Baedeker target, and its bombing was no mean psychological blow. All Britain reeled from the shock. It was as if Germany was telling us, 'We may be losing, but we can still hurt you and that's what we intend to do. Maximally. It isn't over yet.'

And indeed there was almost a year to go before her defeat brought an end to the sufferings on both sides. Meanwhile, the desperate savagery of the endgame continued – till May 1945.

Christmas

Throughout my childhood, Christmas Eve was undeniably the most marvellous day of the year, its magic unequalled even by the Big Day itself. The sheer joy of expectation outdid the actual event. Anticipation had at last reached its climax after building up over months. This was It. By stark contrast, Boxing Day, which ushers in the season of theatrical entertainments, was the year's worst day. Utter anticlimax. Who wants pantomimes? No amount of them could counteract the horrible feeling of 'it's all over'. The marvellousness had gone, like a comet on its appointed way, not to return for another twelve months.

I could never understand when Mother exclaimed, as she often did, 'I'm so glad when Christmas is over!' Incomprehensible! To me, that is. Of course, since I didn't have to do anything – just take, take, take. Whereas for everyone else it was give, give, give – including, generously, of their time and energy. And they just had to do all that; there was absolutely no choice. Not to observe Christmas – was that an option? When the whole nation was geared to it – even Jews, atheists, you name it. I was reminded powerfully of this decades later, when I saw the same applied exactly to Ramadan in Muslim countries. Not to observe it? There wasn't a shred of an option. 'When in Rome.'

The colossal Christmas efforts always began months beforehand. Preparing the cake alone took weeks. Not to mention presents – planning them, budgeting for them, window-shopping for them. One of my friends even started buying them as early as March – if she saw a suitable gift for anyone, she'd snap it up and store it away. As for cards – by mid-August the shops were already awash with them. As for writing them, and the accompanying annual letter (which, strangely enough, seems to have become more de rigueur now than it was then) – better get that chore off your chest by Halloween at the latest. Or else, it's a guilt trip for you – the people you haven't contacted – their cards/missives are invariably the first to drop through your letter box.

Ignore Christmas? You've gotta be kidding.

***

Particular Christmases – with their Eves – stand out sharply in my memory. Pride of place going to that wedding on 24th December 1933. I was three-and-a-half; we had moved to Potters Bar, from Wood Green, just a few months before. In fact, our taking possession of 301 Mutton Lane coincided exactly with Hitler's taking possession of Germany. Furthermore, that Christmas Eve is a date on record in literature – on that very day, Patrick Leigh Fermor was setting out on foot along the Rhine Valley – greeted by swastika-flaunting enthusiasts for Nazism – on his marathon slog to Constantinople, as he chronicles in his famous account of that journey. I know exactly what we were doing while he was doing that: having a whale of a time! At the wedding, the nuptials of Elsie and Jack. They had postponed getting married for some years so that Elsie could go on working and help support me, Daddy having lost his job in the Depression. I only learned about this in 1991, a long time after they had all passed on, from my cousin their daughter. It was one of the many sacrifices they joyfully made for me throughout my childhood and indeed throughout my life – just as when I was a toddler, when my parents broke up, they were there for me, so they were when my own marriage fell apart.

For decades I could recall that wedding scene at St Mary's, The Walk, Potters Bar. But now, more than seventy years on, it's more a case of 'recalling recalling'. I used to have that memory crystal clear, like it was yesterday. Now it's more than a tad blurred. However, it's all preserved vividly in photos. I never went to that church again but in a way revisited it when, a few years ago, BBC TV took us inside for a memorial service for victims of the Potters Bar rail crash, broadcast worldwide.

The wedding reception was held at Bridge House. I don't know if John Morris's family had already taken it over. And another 'memorised memory' pops up – me with my potty clamped to my bottom (Granny dealing so competently with that aspect of all my toddler outings). Oddly, what I retain is a view of myself, a backview, moreover – seeing myself as others must have seen me, rather than the scene from my point of view. Incidentally I have retained exactly the same impression of a similar incident at the Briggs home in Wood Green – one of our frequent visits there. A backview of me, potty-clamped – seeing what others saw, not what I myself must have been looking at. Funny thing, memory.

Like most families, it was our tradition to have the festive meal at home. But at least twice, we deviated from that. Once, we celebrated at Lyons Corner House, in Regent Street, which in those days attracted the middle classes like a magnet for all sorts of functions. This was my first glimpse of the heart of my native city for yes, that's what London is: I was born there, albeit in the suburbs (Wood Green), though raised in Potters Bar. I reckon that confers on me a sort of dual citizenship.

I was intrigued by what I saw of our capital city. The massive, tall, grey buildings. Their greyness was unexpected. As for their height – some five or six storeys! Skyscrapers! Never before seen the likes of them. There was nothing like that in Mutton or Darkes Lane! Lyons Corner House too was a revelation, with all its previously unencountered delicacies; of these, what took my fancy most was – guess what? Rolls and butter! And it's still my favourite to this day!

Another year when we were booked at the Corner House, on Christmas morning I was found to have a temperature. I used to get frightful colds as an infant and only a tonsillectomy put a stop to them. Dilemma! Consternation! To go or not to go? No Plan B in the offing? No such thing as home delivery then. No Kentucky Chicken or MacDonalds – those much-maligned but undeniable solvers of problems. I can't recall what the outcome was. Not going would have spoiled everyone else's Christmas – but then little Timmy's health would surely have been the first consideration in everyone's minds. Maybe I serendipitously perked up? I do hope so for everyone's sake!

So, I come to the most memorable outing of all – not in town but at a nearby hostelry, 'The Three White Swans' on the Great North Road, near Brookmans Park. This was a magnificent event. Along with a superb meal (rolls and butter galore) well organised entertainment was laid on. The MC introduced himself as 'Uncle Fitz'; he encouraged audience participation and urged me to strut my stuff – which I did with aplomb. I was four. What a kick I got out of rendering 'Alice Blue Gown', a ditty I'd recently learned at home. It was ideal for this occasion. Like a pro I warbled:

In my sweet little Alice blue gown
when I first wandered down into town
I was both proud and shy
As I caught every eye
And in every shop window, I primped, passing by.

*"In the manner of fashion I'd frown
And the world seemed to smile all around
Till it wilted, I wore it.
I'll always adore it –
My sweet little Alice blue gown!*

I didn't know what 'primped' meant but not to worry! It brought the house down. What did Shirley Temple have that I didn't? This was my first venture into showbiz and, almost, my last. The following year, having started school, I actually starred in an end-of-term play that had the whole of Potters Bar in thrall – people in the audience were asking, 'Who is she?' Mummy sitting amongst them must have been chuffed to say the least. Stardom looked like being my destiny. But then, inexplicably, came the red face/twitching nerve syndrome, triggering such stage fright that kept me off the boards for many years to come. Though not, I'm glad to say, forever.

At the Three White Swans they begged me for encores but Uncle Fitz was a fair MC and had to let others have their turn, and so they did, giving vent to, among other things, various seasonal staples. Many of these everyone knew by heart those days; people seemed to have absorbed them with their mothers' milk. Not so nowadays. It's a pity. Kids and adults alike are missing out on a heritage if they've never heard, much less learned, such gems as the following: (No prizes for filling in the blanks)

Christmas Day in the Workhouse

*It was Christmas Day in the workhouse
The day of all the……
Their hearts were full of gladness
And their stomachs full of………………*

*In came the workhouse master
To whitewash all the…………………
He wished them a Merry Christmas
But they only answered………………*

*The master he grew angry
And swore by all the……………*

171

They should have no Christmas pudding
The dirty lot of…………
Then up spoke a brave old pauper
Who'd fought in the Khyber…………
We don't want your Christmas pudding
you can stick it up your……………

I cannot resist adding here a related ditty, also by that most prolific of bards, Anon.

In days of old when knights were bold
and paper was not invented
they wiped their…………
On blades of………………
And went away contented.

It wouldn't have been very appropriate, would it, for the Alice Blue Gown starlet to render either of these as encores? 'Timmy' was a precocious brat – but there are limits.

***

Fast forward to the mid-40s and 'Timmy', alias I, had evolved into a mid-teenager. Already working; earning a living, – a pittance but *Deo gratias* I could live on it – at Harrods, in their book department and library. To be near this, I boarded throughout the week at a Spanish convent in Kensington, while returning for weekends to Potters Bar or Palmers Green, Elsie's new abode (part of what you might call 'greater Southgate'). At the convent I gained an unforgettable, truly indelible, impression of Spain – including inter multi alia how Christmas is observed there – in many ways very differently from in England.

To take home for the festive days the nuns gave me ample amounts of seasonal goodies which they themselves had made – they too had been flat out for weeks of preparation. And not only cooking. Practising special hymns in their chapel – they invited me to join in and for a while I was the only non-nun in the choir. It delighted me to discover Spanish Christmas carols, my favourite being one about the Three Wise Kings – *Los Santos Reyes Magos,* how they followed the splendid star (*la splendida estrella*) on their way to Belen (Bethlehem). Like much of the Spanish and Latin music I learned and sang in that chapel, I have never heard these pieces anywhere else before or since, and I've recorded them 'for posterity' in case posterity is interested – I reckon it should be.

Of course I tried hard not to miss on the wireless the Festival of Nine Lessons and Carols from Kings College Cambridge, on Christmas Eve. But there was another less well known musical must for that day – and that was playing a certain Caruso record. It marked the last time he appeared on stage on 24th December 1921 at the Met, it so happened, in Halévy's 'La Juive' the aria being 'Rachel, quand du Seigneur'. Playing this became an intrinsic part of my Noël observances. Ardent opera buff that I had now become, I was starting a collection of discs. I have some of them still, the old 78's, bless them!

Furthermore, being so much influenced by the nuns and their world, I felt I should go to midnight mass; that year (1947) one was held at the Ritz cinema in Potters Bar. Rosemary came with me, as she so often did to my kind of things (whereas I never went to hers – such as cricket at Lords of which she was such a fervent devotee). Later the Ritz underwent another metamorphosis into another kind of temple – this time one of Mammon, to wit a Tesco store.

I feel I shouldn't conclude this piece on Christmas without some reference to Santa Claus. As a little'un I was a firm believer in him. One holiday time (1937) we had relatives staying so our big bedroom upstairs, usually occupied by Mummy and me, was given over to them. I had to sleep in the little downstairs bedroom (afterwards sanctified by the fact that Granny died there). Because such a lot of exciting activity was going on, unique to that night, I couldn't settle to sleep and kept getting up – getting in everyone's way. Exasperated, they told me, 'Now go to bed and stay there – otherwise Santa Claus won't come.' So horrified was I by that possibility I didn't dare get up to go the bathroom when I desperately needed to spend a penny. I struggled to hold it – to no avail, the penny had to be spent. But – Santa came all the same!

And it wasn't the only time he called on me personally – not by a long chalk. One year in early December the front door bell rang; I opened it and who should be standing there but Santa himself. Dressed in a red robe (it bore an uncanny resemblance to Mummy's red dressing gown) and complete with white whiskers and beard.

He asked me, 'Are you Iris Briggs?' Speechless, I nodded in assent. He went on, 'What would you like for Christmas?'

I could barely stammer but I managed to ask, 'Please, Santa, could I have a drawing book?' A modest request but that was truly one of my favourite things – like rolls and butter.

And sure enough, it came. There it was, on Christmas morning – not in a stocking, I was much too spoilt and greedy to be content with that, but in a pillow case. And on it was written, 'To Iris, with love from Santa Claus'. But what struck me most about that was – his handwriting. It was remarkably like Granddad's! What an amazing coincidence!

Dormitory Town?

'Dormitory town' is a phrase often used to describe Potters Bar. In my view, it's wildly inaccurate. You don't go there just to sleep. You go there to live. In fact, you could have a very full, rich life without ever leaving its confines, day or night. However, there were two occasions when, courtesy of Granddad and Doris, I was able to offer 301 as a place for bed, and bit of breakfast.

The first was The Great Gigli Happening. As related elsewhere, as soon as the war was over, to my immense delight London was opened up to the stars of Italian (and German) opera who, throughout the years of conflict had been inaccessible, 'on the other side'. Many of their compatriots, resident in UK, had been interned as enemy aliens. Gigli himself, more than 'arguably' the greatest tenor of those times, was among the first to be so welcomed back – for a performance of 'La Bohème' at Convent Garden. A charming bonus was that his daughter Rina played opposite him as Mimi; no mean soprano in her own right, she was worthy and qualified to partner her illustrious dad*. Of course, I could not possibly forego the chance to see this more than dream come true, something about which I'd fantasised for so long – often hoping against hope. Ever since I'd fallen in love, for life, with this kind of music, I'd longed for London to be the centre of it again – but never dared imagine this would come about so soon.

Though it would mean queueing probably for a whole day and maybe a night too, and although I was barely convalescent from flu (still on sick leave from Harrods), I had no choice but to go and get those tickets. Accordingly, one fine late autumn morning I rushed out very early from the convent and got myself to Covent Garden by 7 am. I found the queue already surrounding the opera house. Among the queuers I was surprised to see a maths master from Southgate County

---

* She also gave a radio concert; I was specially impressed by her rendering of Solveig's Song – and by the fact that she'd included it in her programme. Not confining herself to the bel canto repertoire but also singing pieces well loved by a northern audience.

– not dear musical Mr Armstrong but another who once had reprimanded me for being a mathematical dunce. So I was hardly on his wavelength and was therefore astonished to see him here – thus proving himself to be a fellow human being after all.

I remained in the queue all day – it was 4th November 1946. Despite my bladder problem; I was still having to cope with that and doing so by the skin of my teeth – to resort to a mixed metaphor. So it seemed little short of a miracle that for hours I felt no need to urinate. Talk about mind over matter! Positive thinking! Only once, in the late afternoon at that, did I feel that – just in case – I should ask someone to safeguard my place in the queue while I repaired to a public loo at Leicester Square.

Throughout that day we aficionados stood there and watched an entire shop front being painted from beginning to end. An atmosphere of extreme camaraderie prevailed; fellow-queuers seemed as dear to each other as next of kin. Then – at approximately 6 pm, when we found ourselves at long last getting near the box office, the atmosphere dramatically changed. From cuddly to cut-throat. So fierce was the competition for those tickets, one felt one might kill to lay hands on them. I didn't go that far but I did resort to mild violence – ruthlessly elbowing, pushing and shoving the surrounding throng of rivals, holding them at bay, staving them off till I managed to get my hot sticky fingers on four of those precious bits of paper – enough for Rosemary and me plus two convent comrades, for the opening night.

Because of the nuns' strictly observed closing hours – you had to be in by ten (did they fondly imagine that anything untoward we might get up to could only be done after that?) we had perforce to spend the night somewhere else. Potters Bar it had to be: Granddad and Doris kindly welcomed my guests as their own, and we all duly dossed down around 1 am! Back to work in the morning! For me Harrods beckoned (my sick leave now over) with its clocking-in system and I just made it – thanks to the 29 bus and the Piccadilly Line.

There was one other occasion when I personally validated the "dormitory town" label. That was when we invited Madge Smythe to spend a Sunday chez nous – like Lily Andrews and Lalla Scruby, Doris's close friends, sometimes did. Again, my guest was their guest. What better proof that this was indeed my very own home! How I wish there could have been more of such lovely happenings – but, alas, not very long after this Granddad passed on, and our 301 ceased to exist. The family agreed that it be sold – only Doris dissented, urging that 'It could be a home for Iris!' Bless her! For Iris herself, in her naïveté and downright ignorance, simply didn't grasp the value of what she had – a dear, dear abode she should have clung on to with might and main. Instead, she was only too keen to get her hands on things she didn't have – cash, to buy pretty clothes, to travel to Italy…

So we all left. Never to return. It was destiny. But not dormitory town.

Postscript

About maths masters

It was odd how they made a special mark on our memory. Another example is Mr Knowles, the head of that department at Southgate County. He was a Potters Bar man – his was the very first house you'd see, on your right as you came into town from the direction of Stagg Hill. (When the M25 was installed, that row of dwellings was pulled down). He stands out in my mind because of his comment on our obtuse reaction to the *pons asinorum* theorem, 'No wonder Pythagoras threw himself off a rock!'

E = MC – What?

Mine weren't the only maths masters who seemed to dog our steps during the war and post-war years. Mother's did, too. She and her sister Elsie had been at Wood Green County School before WWI; she'd been taught maths there by one PK Thompson. By the 1940s, he was well and truly retired and chose to settle in the vicinity of Forestdale; he often strolled past our gate, accompanied by his better half.

'Did he know all about squaring the circle?' I enquired of Mama. 'Well, he squared her circle all right', was her typical riposte.

***

Elsie too had a guru at Wood Green County – her English master there was a certain Christopher Bush. Teaching was his day-job but by vocation he was a whodunnit writer. In those days he was just beginning to become known. Though he never rivalled Agatha and her like he did make a name for himself with a series, *The Case of the*…this, that or the other. These books, some dozen or so of them, formed part of the staple fare in Boots the Chemist's library.

He was no absent-minded "creative" type – in class he disciplined the kids quite severely. At WGC those days, as at Cranborne in mine, "talking" was viewed as the cardinal sin, followed closely by 'not paying attention', especially turning around to chat with those seated behind. In response to one of his pupils doing precisely that, writer Bush hurled a chalk at him, with the admonition, 'Remember Lot's wife!' Elsie remembered that forever and relayed it to me.

It would seem that we tend to forget most of the stuff our gurus strove with such zest to din into our skulls. While we forever recall this or that odd thing about them personally, their 'funny little ways.' Well, that too is, I suppose, a sort of immortality – and, I guess, one that said gurus might well prefer.

Don't Slate the Slate

'Did you say State schools?'

'No, I said slate schools.'

'What on earth do you mean by that?'

'I'll explain.'

Walking home from Cranborne with Daddy one afternoon. A rare occurrence, on several counts. Firstly 'cos it must have been Saturday, the day for his "me" visit, i.e. weekend when we'd normally be off school. But in the early months of the war attendance schedules were adjusted; we had to go in shifts so there'd always be enough room for those present in the shelters.

Walking home with Daddy! Most of the kids had never even seen my father and probably some of them doubted that I had one. Especially since, on being required to fill in some form giving parents' address, I'd boasted to Mr Sims (yes, boasted was the word) in front of the whole class, 'My father doesn't live with us!' I'd wanted to show him and them. 'We're different! We're interesting!' (Possibly being illegitimate would have been even more so.) 'We're not ordinary'– number-one sin in my eyes – 'like all these run-of-the-mill brats.'

Even so, paradoxically, I felt it was fine for them to get the message, by actually seeing him, holding my hand moreover, taking me home. 'So Iris Briggs has got a dad after all. A dad who cares about her.' I wanted my bread buttered both sides!

Another striking aspect of that Saturday walk home was that Rosemary's pa was strolling along with us. He too was rarely to be seen in Potters Bar, since he was in the army, stationed abroad. An unfaultable alibi – nothing in the least dubious or weird or questionable about it – so my dad could have one like that too. What went for the Randalls should go for the Briggses. The two men were having a good old natter. Yet another rarity was, Rosemary and I were brandishing slates. We'd recently been issued with them in the cause of saving paper. These newly acquired tools seemed more like toys, each with its own stylus and little sponge; they were quite a sensual pleasure to use, to handle and just look at, as well as being a novelty.

Slates. They struck me as being a link with Shakespeare. I could more easily picture him carrying a slate than an exercise book as he 'crept like a snail unwillingly to school.' And indeed our grandparents if not our parents too had used them – they'd been the thing then, part of the standard school equipment like, say, satchels. In fact exercise books were relatively recent innovations.

Such reflections prompted me to peer even further into the past, spawning a parody of my own:

In days of old
When knights were bold
And slates were not invented
They did their sums
On people's bums
provided they consented!

Deskmates

When we left Cranborne for the very last time we called at Mr Sims' office to bid formal adieu to our Head. 'We' being a delegation of that favourite, special 1A – Margaret Wood, Rosemary and I, Derek and John, and one or two others. It was the right thing to do. And we did it. And our Head, too, said all the right things, like 'keep the flag flying'. That may sound corny today, far from cool, a bit Sir Henry Newboltish – 'play up, play up, and play the game.' Call me old-fashioned but I relish all that and revere it too. If it was jingoistic, so be it – that was justified. Those days Hitler was within sight, just across the Channel.

After leaving and moving on to secondary school we tried to maintain our links with Cranborne and were planning to set up an Old Scholars' Association – we got as far as drawing up some rules and buying some badges, but inevitably it fizzled out. A bit like the 'gang' – sorry, 'guild'. We didn't like leaving our alma mater – it deserves that title, albeit only a primary school. But no school is more important than that – the one where you learn to read and write as well as the basics of socialisation.

However, one can't stay in the kindergarten forever, either literally or figuratively. And not very long after this, one of our farewell delegation did indeed move on – to a higher plane. He was Brian Carter, one of the brightest of the boys. He figures in the last school photo taken on the playing fields before they were dug up to make air-raid shelters. And he also appears in earlier classroom groups – he worked his way up the school. But not long after our formal taking leave of the Head it was Brian's destiny to pass away from this life. That was extremely sad for all of us; I'm sure Derek felt it very keenly as Brian was his deskmate. I'm sure he'll remember him forever.

At the secondary school too there was a happening like that – a classmate called Mary Holt; she was an enthusiastic and generous contributor to the form magazine I ran, and took part in our discussions à la Brains Trust, for which we commandeered our domestic science lessons. She posed a question for our consideration, 'Is there a purpose to the universe?' We eagerly debated that, paying much more attention to it than to the leek-and-potato pie we were supposed to be cooking.

There was a time lasting several months when I used to stroll around the playground arm-in-arm with Mary before going into Assembly. I vividly remember the smell of her raincoat. One day she fell and sustained a wound which turned septic. No penicillin then or other antibiotics; although Sir Alexander Fleming had discovered them some years previously, the pharmaceutical industry hadn't yet placed them on general sale. So the sepsis took its course. It was a sad day indeed for the whole school when Mary quit this life – unbearably sad and I can't easily write about it.

Her mortal remains were repatriated to her native St. Helens in Lancashire; I always think of her whenever this town is mentioned in the sports news, as it often is, a leading football team being from there. Auxerre likewise features frequently in such bulletins and always makes me think of Vercingetorix whom Caesar vanquished there and subsequently executed. I am so sorry about that and ardently wish he hadn't done it. I used to have quite heated arguments about this with another deskmate of mine, Liliane Diévart, the only French pupil at Southgate County and I was very pleased that she happened to be seated next to me. Vercingetorix was her great hero, but Caesar was mine. She considered Caesar's act a war crime, but I tried to point out, '*Autres temps, autres moeurs.*' There was no Geneva convention those days, or anything like it. And, anyway, I can't help it, Caesar exerts such a powerful hold on my emotions, even after twenty centuries, that I have to overlook his faults, albeit serious ones.

Liliane was staying in England with her mother; I believe her father was in France fighting in the Resistance, like Pierre Roche. She herself was presented to General de Gaulle. I've lost touch with her but, like all those with whom one shares a desk, she is never to be forgotten.

Around that time – about the middle of the war – Winston Churchill went down with pneumonia and received a wonder drug that had newly been developed but, like the antibiotics, was not yet generally available. It was called M & B 693. Mother read avidly about all such medical matters in the newspapers and her nursing magazines and relayed the information to me. I recall her stating her opinion, 'Stevie's [my baby brother's] life is more valuable than Churchill's.' Another snippet of Churchilliana she conveyed to me was how he said, around that time, 'We have in our possession a weapon too terrible to imagine' – or words to that effect. 'Nothing like it has ever been used before.' He was of course referring to the atomic bomb; we remembered his words after it had been dropped on Hiroshima and Nagasaki. If he had known about and approved of the intention to use it, he shared the blame with Truman and the pilots who actually bombed those cities. Small wonder if Churchill is viewed very differently in Japan and Germany from in his own country. One man's war hero is another man's war criminal. *N'est-ce pas, Liliane?*

'War is the absolute evil' – a line from a poem by my beloved Rosemary written around Hiroshima time. And one thinks not only of WWII but of WWI. If the former was indeed unavoidable, not so the latter. Politicians should have exerted every muscle to stop – the trenches, Somme, Passchendaele, Ypres. Gas. I think of the Finlayson brothers, their names inscribed on the roll of honour at Southgate County. 'To the Fallen.' Fighting the Kaiser – in the name of what? The Finlaysons were Daddy's schoolmates. I like to think that maybe one of them was his deskmate too.

Dancing in the Streets

Dancing in the streets has never been a particularly English activity. But all the rules were broken for VE Day. VE Night, rather. 'Victory in Europe.' Could it really be true? We'd won the war? It was all over? Bar the shouting, yes. Bar Japan, no. Hiroshima was yet to come – though not far off.

Could it really be true? No more air-raid warnings? No more fear? Hitler might use gas? He might, and did, use pilotless planes. No more V1s and V2s?

'When they sound the last All Clear
How happy, my darling, we'll be.
When they turn on the lights
And the dark, lonely nights
I Are only a memory.

You can say that again. 'Cos when we sang it, singing along with Vera Lynn or in the school shelters, in the depths of the Blitz, we couldn't really believe it. Half scolding ourselves, 'Wishful thinking'. But sometimes, occasionally, wishful thinking comes true. Here was just such a case. They had sounded the Last All Clear.

It was all over. We'd won the war. So – what to do about it? Well, no need to think that through – just surge into the streets. And dance and dance and dance.

Forestdale and Mutton Lane and Laurel Avenue. All those streets throughout the length and breadth of the land wherever bombs or landmines or rockets had fallen, wherever people had sheltered in their Andersons or Morrisons or slept, taking a chance, in their beds. It was all over! No more need to balance your gasmask in a certain way on the chair beside your bed before you'd feel safe enough to drift into sleep. It was all over! The only feeling remotely like it was when you wake after a particularly horrible nightmare with inexpressible relief. 'Thank God – it was a nightmare and it's passed.'

Surge into the streets, and dance – with the first partner who comes to hand. Even a Belgian refugee! But not Mr Fujihito – he, understandably perhaps, kept a low profile. For once not 'joining in'. Though he'd surely earned the right to do so. No denying he'd done his bit like the rest of us. Nevertheless – understandable if 'deep down' he had mixed feelings.

The first partner who came to hand in my case was Mr Lambrini. Italian, yes! Enemy alien, no! Several generations back his folk had moved here and they'd stayed on. He and I danced and danced and danced – me a teenager, he verging on his 80s – like Toscanini who, believe it or not, was scheduled to be in London soon, conducting at the Albert Hall. Plus a bevy of top opera singers, led by Gigli, at Covent Garden. Dream come true! Paradise regained! No more cause to fear for the safety of cultural monuments. Let alone human beings. Or for that matter pussy cats like Natushka – be they here or in Italy, or Germany, or Russia.

We danced and no doubt we could have danced all night – as Julie Andrews was later to exhort us. Thanks to her discoverer, Der Old Vic – Vic Oliver. Here's a case where the protegée outshone the mentor – but he'd never have minded one iota, only too proud and delighted for her. So I danced and Mr Lambrini danced, and Mummy and Stepdaddy too – the lot of us, there in Forestdale. 'Victory in Europe.' Bought at a price. But those who'd paid it, like Pat Garland and his brothers, would have been the gladdest of the glad, to see us all celebrate, see us all so happy.

A few months later, it was time for VJ Night. 'Victory over Japan.' And, significantly perhaps, there was no dancing. Though there was a big event to mark it in Broomfield Park. Observances were more solemn. This time Mr Fujihito kept an even lower profile. And that was even more understandable. In spite of all his being 'integrated', with his Daily Telegraph, bowler hat and rolled umbrella, despite being *'plus Brit que les Brits'* – surely he felt terrible about Hiroshima and Nagasaki. Because we did too.

Thomas Freshwater Briggs, 1858–1948

My paternal grandfather, Thomas Freshwater Briggs, whom we always called 'Tom', lived through WWII but it wasn't the only war he lived through, by any means. Or even the last. There was Korea, remember? The first, believe it or not, was the American Civil War. He was born in 1858, three years before it broke out. And only ten years after Emily Brontë died.

The mid-nineteenth century. It marked the end of an extremely long period of the human story – in fact, from its very start in pre-historic times, right up to the Industrial Revolution, when everything was stood on its head. Thus, people like the Brontës and their contemporaries were subject to exactly the same hazards, particularly health hazards, as the Pharaohs. No antiseptics; no anaesthetics either. Came Pasteur and immunisations were on their way; with the Curies, so was radiation therapy. Granddad Tom himself had had smallpox and bore the marks of it. And it wasn't only health that underwent 'revolution'. Transport, too – railways were the bellwether, Emily and her sisters shrewdly buying shares. Then in due course came cars. Planes, sputniks etc. Communications were utterly transformed. Photography, telephones, radio, cinema…Anyone born in the early part of Victoria's reign who survived till the latter part of it straddled in their lifetime a before-and-after divide as crucial as the one between BC and AD. Part I of mankind's biography had reached its closing chapter; Part II was about to be written.

Granddad Tom was a child of the nineteenth century just as I am one of the twentieth. A treasured photo I have of us together – he about seventy, me rising two, he embracing me in his garden at Wood Green – this photo exactly symbolises for me the nineteenth century embracing the twentieth.

Like Granddad Rodwell, he was an exceptional person. But in a very different way. An engineer, devoted both to the theoretical side of that discipline and also to the nitty-gritty. He like doing hands-on stuff – and paid a price for it, since he lost two fingers of his left hand in an experiment. In his garden he had his workshop with its stock of fascinating instruments. I used to peer at them bewildered – I hadn't a clue what any of them were for. In his garden too he had a splendid fuschia; it reigned supreme in a prominent position, queening it over all the other flowers there. I always paid my respects to it. I never see a fuschia without remembering him.

He continued with his work well into his seventies. By an odd coincidence I once bumped into him in Potters Bar, at the end of Cranborne Road where it peters out at the railway bridge beyond which lie the golf links. I didn't often happen to be wandering around that part of town and had no idea he was there. With him was a team of workers; they were taking care of a steam roller, one of his special interests.

My mother had foretold that he would live to be ninety; I was powerfully reminded of this when I watched his casket being lowered, inscribed with his name and dates, 'Thomas Freshwater Briggs, 1858–1948'. He loved my mother very much and was greatly distressed by the split-up of my parents' marriage – and the installation of a 'consort' as my father's partner. It was hard for Granddad Tom being part of that uncomfortable household, especially after my grandmother, Gertrude Briggs, died. He didn't speak about these traumatic subjects; he didn't need to. I knew full well what his feelings were.

He cared such a lot about me. He would come to meet me after school and walk home with me as far as Forestdale. But he didn't come in – much as he surely would have loved to meet up with Mother again. Probably he hesitated to do so because of Step – embarrassed, perhaps, and unsure of the reception he'd get. Thinking that here there well might be another unfriendly 'consort'. I should have reassured him: Step was a very decent person and would have received him pleasantly. But I didn't speak up – one of my long list of regrets (no Piaf, me, far from it). Well, I was only a kid, not possessed of much wisdom.

Granddad Tom also came to visit me in hospital when I went in for that check-up operation – retrograde pyelogram – to try to trace the cause of my bladder problem. He was eighty-nine. I was so thrilled when I caught sight of him coming along the ward! So appreciative he had made the effort, the darling!

By that time he had been placed in an Old People's Home – a euphemism if ever there was one. It was a most uncongenial place; he told me how some of the inmates had 'the manners of pigs'. It upset me that he should be subjected to such horrible company. But perhaps he had chosen it in preference to that of the consort. I'm so glad that, on my visit there, I took him a peach – the most beautiful fruit I could find. I know he must have enjoyed it – and the proof it was of how I too cared.

How I wish we'd been together more! We had such a lot to share, such a lot in common. Among many other things, books. He had a lot of very interesting and unusual ones, including an anthology of epitaphs and a dictionary of Cornish – a rarity indeed. I wonder what happened to them. Probably Daddy, or his brother Arthur, inherited them (his other brother Vernon, having predeceased Tom) but after they too died, I was already living abroad and these books didn't come my way. How I would have treasured them.

How I would have treasured, too, more time with beloved Tom. Even so, the little time we did share was immensely valuable, immensely meaningful. We may not have talked that much, but the things unsaid were themselves conversation aplenty.

Postscript

The American Civil War wasn't the only civil war to impinge upon the Briggs family. Another was our home-grown variety (1642–1649) between Parliament (Roundheads) under Oliver Cromwell and royalists (Cavaliers) supporting King Charles I. Huntingdon, situated virtually in the centre of England, the Briggs's native place, was in the heart of Roundhead territory; a statue of Cromwell lords it over the centre of the town to this day.

In the early nineteenth century my great-grandfather Francis Briggs ran a hostelry there called 'The Old Spare Rib'. It was a stop for passengers on stage coaches going north and south. Such as Dorothy Wordsworth bound for her visit to the Lambs in London. On her return journey to her family at Grasmere in the Lake District, travelling with her was the professor of Arabic at Cambridge; I guess 'change at Huntingdon' was on his schedule and possibly they both made use of The Old Spare Rib, at least to spend a penny and perhaps to spend the night.

Daddy and I were talking about all this as we strolled around London one day. At that point in Whitehall where King Charles had stepped out to his execution Daddy remarked, 'I think old Oliver went too far.'

At Potters Bar I reckon we must have been in the Cavalier rather than the Roundhead camp – I deduce as much from the curiously named church in Mutton Lane, between our home and the Cranborne estate of 'King Charles the Martyr'. 'Martyr to what?' you may ask. Answer, the concept of the Divine Right of Kings. This was High Church; I don't recall attending any service there, but sometimes as I passed it I heard the lovely treble of my schoolmate Horace Norburn practising his solos. There are one or two other churches similarly named scattered throughout the country, but none of course in Huntingdon.

Charles and Mary Lamb

I often think of Charles and Mary Lamb when I picture Potters Bar as it must have been some two hundred years ago. They are among the few known personalities associated with it, who ever visited it or mentioned it in their writings. And I wonder what drew them there in the first place. Perhaps they'd read about Wyllyotts Manor in Domesday Book and 'done' it without benefit of tourist guides. Or perhaps they'd plodded out to the site of the Battle of Barnet where, in 1475, Warwick the Kingmaker 'met his Waterloo', and HG Wells, still far in the future for the Lambs, made his Martians land in 'The War of the Worlds': but there's nothing much to see in that vicinity – except, nearby famous Watling Steet...survivor of the Roman road network, heading for the Midlands. In the town itself, the Lambs would doubtless have been curious about the Church of King Charles the Martyr but that too had not yet been built in their day. It must just have been the nice long walk! They certainly wouldn't have wanted to live there. I recall how Charles regarded nearby 'darkest Enfield', where he was forced to reside for a while, as ultima Thule; among his many peeves about it was that he'd had to wait ages for his Sunday newspapers. So what about Potters Bar? Whatever...Go there he and his sister certainly did.

On the far right of the Mutton Lane cemetery as you go in through the lych gate is the old original part of this burial ground. A spill-over from the already filled-up churchyards on the High Street, aka the Great North Road, or the A1000, going towards Brookmans Park. (Now who, I wonder, was Brookman? Like Darke (or Darkes) a forgotten personality of past times who none the less has bequeathed his name to his native place. Huge houses of worship stood along that great highway; they had already long since been abandoned when we arrived in 1933. Here in the first established part of the new cemetery lie those who, in the late eighteenth and early nineteenth centuries lived in Potter's Bar (as Lamb writes it – when did the apostrophe fall out of use? – sometime between his day and ours.) These citizens lived through Trafalgar and yes, Waterloo, and saw

Queen Victoria come to the throne. Contemporaries of Charles and Mary, they might well have bumped into them on this or that weekend foray of theirs – his blessed weekend escape from desk-bound drudgery at the East India Company's office in the City. Believe it or not, he and his sister would eagerly trek out as far as here from their home in Islington. And back! On foot! No London Underground then, no Piccadilly – or any other – Line. Trains themselves had barely come into existence, though Emily Brontë was already looking into railway investment possibilities (and learning to use a gun!) There were no such things as buses either, no double deckers or No. 29 route. Even no bikes. And they didn't so much as avail themselves of gee-gees.

It was very much a matter of uphill and downdale. Stagg Hill was as steep then as it ever was in my time – steeper, probably, as it does mysteriously seem to grow shallower with each passing decade. On the lines of 'when we were small and Christmas trees were tall.' The Lambs had only Shanks's pony to rely upon for every step of their way and back. Yet they considered themselves softies compared with their pals the Wordsworths with their endless Lake District marathons. Knackering as it must have been for Charles and Mary, yet the unpolluted air must have done them a power of much-needed good – even more than it does their fellow Londoners today. They could hardly have emitted a single footprint of CO_2 between them, even in the heart of the City. They must have considered the colossal effort of escape worthwhile – one day off in seven incomparably better than nowt – to the extent of equipping themselves with a big basket of victuals. Of course, preparing its contents would have been Mary's job, just as preparing the Wordsworths' ditto would have been Dorothy's – the men to be on no account distracted from their all-important scribblings.

However, being gentlemen, they would at least have helped carry the load, perhaps single-handed or perhaps swinging it between them. Tucked in among the goodies would have been a serviceable carving knife and no doubt a smattering of spoons and forks (a far from innocuous accessory – see below*). A glass or two and a bit of napery.

Popping in at this or that eatery (like for instance, Bridge House of John Morris fame) – was it already in situ then? – or some earlier version? As for the bridge itself, it too maybe was yet to be built, since its raison dêtre – the railway

---

* Madly hurling forks – a phrase prominent in the official account of Mary's fatal attack upon her mother as the table was laid for a meal, one day in the 1790s

– wasn't yet constructed. Though Mutton Lane was certainly there and must have been for centuries. In active use moreover. Riding high over the lower-lying fields through which the main-line tunnel was eventually gouged. "Our heroes" might well have ventured into a pub/inn/hostelry to ask mine host or hostess for a table or tablecloth which, very probably, they would have been glad enough to provide – that is, as long as they remained ignorant of the identity of their guests. Once that cat was out of the bag, they could well have had second thoughts – in a big way. Should the merest inkling have seeped through that they were harbouring under their roof a matricidal maniac, complete with carving knife (and a bevy of forks – again, see below) it would have been a very different matter. A mayhem situation, no less. They wouldn't have been able to dial 999 – and no Bobbie Peel within many miles' radius. The best thing they could do would be to barricade themselves in, battening down the hatches, bellowing to clients and neighbours to do likewise. Hoping for the best till help arrived or danger passed.

Poor Charles. Lord David Cecil has recounted his story so poignantly in his superb biography. Most poignant of all, the irony – that quality which Charles prized above all others. The fact that he needed Mary so much more than she needed him – despite the sacrifice of his entire life, his entire happiness, for her, she scarcely seemed to notice when he passed away. In darkest Edmonton, it so happened.

Going over and over the Lambs' story – 'Lambs' Tales', might we not call them? – I never cease to marvel at the liberal attitude of the courts that dealt with that tragedy way back in the 1790s. Electing to entrust Mary to her loving brother's care instead of dooming her to lifelong incarceration in a madhouse. And madhouse meant madhouse – call a spade a spade. That judgement was spectacularly humane – much more so than many being passed down nowadays. But: was it wise? Was it even right? I venture to question that. At any moment Mary might have succumbed to some lapse – the exact antithesis of a 'lucid period' – putting at risk those at close range. Including of course Charles himself and such others as happened to come within orbit – e.g. Dorothy Wordsworth, who shared a bed with her on that so memorable visit to London when the historic Wordsworth/Coleridge/Lamb/Keats dinner took place – and one again wonders what part Mary and Dorothy played in that. Cooks and bottle-washers most probably. Though no mean scribblers themselves, whatever literary urges they might have harboured – stronger, superior perhaps, to those of their menfolk, who knows? In those days for females household duties always had to take precedence over everything else.

Yes, sharing a bed with a proven murderess was no trivial matter, and the courts were to blame for allowing it to happen. Liberal, well-meaning, but nonetheless misguided. Yet – the alternative? Locked away forever in bedlam? Charles's description of her overheard ravings does not make comfortable reading.

'Madness in the family.' A phrase that recurs in Charles's (Elia's) writings. And Mary's wasn't the only case of it among the Lambs. Charles too had been slightly brushed by it and even briefly hospitalised – an experience which, he states, he thoroughly enjoyed: thanks no doubt to its mildness and perhaps its unreality contrasting pleasantly with East India drudgery. A species of holiday!

One is reminded also of their Hertfordshire cousins. How in his early years he'd been smitten by one of them and asked to marry her, but her next of kin had politely though firmly turned him down. 'Madness in the family.' No need to know about DNA – its discovery still far into the future – to realise the hazards involved. And perhaps, the actress to whom he proposed decades later, also knew of that 'taint' and because of it – respectfully, delicately, touched, but equally firmly, rejected him.

Poor Charles.

The Sweetest Soul

'The sweetest soul that ever looked with human eyes.'

So reads the epitaph for Agnes Birrell (Nancy) on the most beautiful of all the monuments in the Mutton Lane cemetery. It's on your left as you go in through the lych gate and walk up the main path leading to the central circle of graves. Hers is a very delicately carved cross, surmounting a square plot. Recorded is the fact that she lived near Bentley Heath, in one of the big houses lying back from the main road – that is, the Great North Road, alias the A1000, that, having briefly been Barnet High Street soon becomes just as briefly that of Potters Bar. She lived there around the turn of the last two centuries, i.e. the nineteenth and twentieth. Trying to picture her, I cannot help but recall the heroines of George Eliot and Elizabeth Gaskell. But there was nothing fictitious about Nancy. A very, very real person, to those who so achingly loved her. If I were an ardent Christian, I'd cross myself every time I pass her so moving memorial. I was shocked when, on my last visit there, in 1991, I found the cross had fallen and was lying on the untended grass of the grave plot. It had already been leaning awry when I'd made another, very brief, visit there some years earlier. Of course, there's nobody left now to take care. Like in the case of the first people whose remains were brought here, over on the far right, way back in Charles Lamb's time, because there was no more room in the big, old churchyards. As the burial grounds gradually fill up, so the caring people themselves pass on, till no one is left.

Whenever I think of this cemetery, which is often, Agnes Birrell (Nancy) unfailingly comes to my mind. I wonder about her, wish I'd known her, wish there were some photographs or other records of her and her life. But that phrase, 'the sweetest soul that ever looked with human eyes' is enough to make me care about her always, and her unwritten tragedy.

If I've reverted a lot to this cemetery throughout this book it's because there's so much there that demands reverting to. And as I wander around, whether in reality or 'in vacant or in pensive mood', my gaze alighting upon this or that sombre patch, certain ideas or images present themselves. Suicide, mental illness, euthanasia – those are some of them. One of Granddad's comrades, a Bowling Club stalwart – I know he pleaded to be released from agony and I'm sure his pleas did not meet with an indifferent response. Then – 'the girl who walked from Warrengate Farm' – did she, or did she not, cry halt to her own suffering? How many others similarly challenged lie nearby? How many soldiered on to a more than bitter end, battling physical or mental ills for which no cures were then known?

I know so many stories about the denizens of this place, some of them heartrending. Sagas of unforgettable sadness. None more so than that of the Deale family. Rosemary Deale was in my cohort at Cranborne – the same age but in a different class. The whole school mourned her tragic passing at age eight, in 1938, from kidney malfunction*. Again, cures were not known (or if they were, they were simply not available) that have become widely dispensed since. Her parents had already lost one baby, called Iris – Rosemary and Iris, namesakes of me and my best friend, and the coincidence gave me a comforting feeling; I felt there was a blessing about it. Their little resting place is guarded by sculpted angels; it lies between our own family plot and that of the German Zeppelin crew. I felt so terribly sorry for their mother and, 'precocious brat' though I was, could yet understand how unutterably precious her remaining child must be. The war came soon after that, with it the bombing, and the already so stricken woman lost her husband in a raid on Kings Cross. Her suffering is over now – it ended in 1976, as I found on my 1991 visit – the Deale family grave, inscribed 'Together at last' is very near the Rodwell one. Though twenty-six years separate the two burials the land here is not filling up as quickly as it used to as cremation has been increasingly preferred in recent decades.

There's so much to provoke deep thought at this sombre yet peaceful scene. Small wonder that, after twelve years of being under psychological pressure to give up my writing I began to feel – prompted by memories of this very place – the power to do it surging back, irresistibly. Thoughts of this cemetery, of those whose remains were brought finally to lie here, inspired and encouraged me.

---

* We had shared a 'boyfriend' – Tony McLeod – a very innocent set-up. After she passed away I didn't see much of him – it was as if he'd lost interest in me. I didn't mind, or when people said: "Rosemary was his sweetheart."

First and foremost of those, of course, were my beloved grandparents, Albert and Florence Rodwell, who gave me the greatest home I've ever had, blessed 301. It wasn't a very long way for them to go from 301 to 709, the number allotted to their resting place. Calling en route at the Baptist Church where Aubrey Argyll DD gave his thoughtful, compassionate sermons and Psalm 23 radiated blessings over all present.

Memories beget other memories. Among my countless recollections of walks with Granddad, my infant hand clutching his elderly one – whenever we happened to pass a funeral cortège he would invariably raise his hat, unfailingly giving the dead their due. But when we ourselves were riding with him on his solemn last journey, I was very shocked, and very hurt, to see a lout in our own Mutton Lane – indeed, at the very 'pivotal point' (see entry so named) not taking the slightest notice as Granddad passed, not giving the slightest sign of respect. I could hardly believe it. What shall I say? Other than 'no comment'.

A final memory. I don't know if I shall ever go to the cemetery again. But when I last did so, in 1991, something quite striking happened. My cousin and her husband had taken me there, with one of my daughters and her children. Of course, since it hadn't been touched for many a long year, resting place no 709 was overgrown with weeds and grasses running wild. My cousin in particular made great efforts to clear away all this so that the names at last shone through: Florence and Albert Rodwell. We had to bid them farewell not knowing when, if ever, we should be able to come there again.

After such a struggle with the undergrowth of course our hands were in need of a wash.

I said, 'Perhaps we could pop in at Bridge House for that' but my cousin remarked, 'I don't think they'd be very keen.' Regardless of the John Morris connection; the hostelry might have changed hands, maybe more than once, since my Cranborne days – mostly probably had, since its name had changed, from 'Bridge House' to 'The Bridge'. Perhaps the present owners wouldn't be even as keen to let us wash our hands there as their way-back predecessors had been to lend a table cloth to the Lambs.

Then the thought struck me, *No need to bother them.* For I remembered. Always, in the past, as we went in through the lych gate, on the right there was a tap – countless times I'd used it, when we'd come to tend the flowers for Granny, planted and cared for so lovingly by Granddad, and later those placed there for him too. I knew exactly where that tap was and led the others in that direction, hoping so much it was still there. I longed to see it again. And – there it was! Telling me, after all those years away, those decades, that more than half a century – 'Here I am! Just like you remember me.' Providing visible, tangible evidence of my enduring link with this hallowed place. I hadn't forgotten it, and it hadn't forgotten me. Just like the Fire Hydrant!

The End